Getting Focused
Staying Focused

A Far Eastern Approach to Sports and Life

BY ALAN JAEGER

"Silence is perhaps the greatest teacher of all."

Printed in the United States of America

ISBN 1881643239
Library of Congress card catalogue number 94-75092
Jaeger, Alan
   Getting Focused, Staying Focused

Editor: Rosalee J. Jaeger
Copy Editor: William Yanes
Cover Design and Graphics: Janice Metz
Typesetting: William Yanes
Cover Photography: Mike Guastella (Back)
Cover Photography: Alan Jaeger (Front)
Public Relations: Jennifer Vides

Griffin Printing
544 West Colorado Street
Glendale, California 91204

Grateful Acknowledgement is made to the legacy of LaoTzu and Alan Watts, whose insight and wisdom served as the inspiration behind the writing of this book. It is also noteworthy that excerpts of the Tao Te Ching are taken from Stephen Mitchell's adaptation (HarperCollins).

DEDICATION

To my Mother, and editor, Rosalee, whose talent, support and direction made this book possible.

To Janice Metz, for turning concepts into beautiful art.

To Jim Vatcher, for, among other things, keeping his eyes open and remaining still in the bright Las Vegas sun!

I would also like to thank the following people, who have all, in their own unique way, given me the support and inspiration to make this book possible:

Joe Adamiak, Tad & Debbie Akin, Jill Androni, Dana Arnold, Travis Arsenault, Fariborz Azhakh, Tom Ball, Roxanne Bastran, Diana Beardsley, Mike Bell, Louis Birdt, Bambi Blitz, Jason Bott, Chris Brown, California Lutheran University (1992, 1993), Billy Carlson, Craig Carlton, Jeremy Carr, The Chatham A's (1992, 1993), The Chatham Athletic Association, Gabe Chavez, The Chavez Family, Jason Cohen, Diane Cooper, Bryan Corey, Steve Dempsey, Nate Dishington, Bob Duca, Eric Duncan, Todd Elliot, The Farbers, Tammy Flaherty, Laia Gasch, Marc Glennie, Griffin Printing, Keith Grunwald, Mike Guastella, Jack Hammond, Lionel Hastings, Mike Haugh, The Heberts, Erik Hiljus, Rich Hill, Jan Holt, Jake Jacobsen, Martin Jaeger, Stuart & Karen Jaeger, Susan Jaeger, "Larry" Jaeger, Stig & Tracy Jantz, Angela Johnson, Mike & Mary Keens, John Klitsner, Mariann Kourfas, David Lamb, Danny Larson, The Las Vegas Stars Baseball Club, Doug Latta, Arlene Lebeitsamer, Anne LeClaire, Jim Lewis, The Lieberthals, Bob Lofrano, The Longs, Roy Lozano, Jay Lucas, Ruth Maier, The Mandell Family, Derrick Manning, Barbara Marron, Erik Martinez, Wally Maynard, The Mearns, The McAdam Family, Dave Mendoza, Tajah Merril, Tom Merril, Rob "Ben" Miles, Herman & Daisy Miller, Dennis Moeller, Shaun Murphy, Bud Murray, John Najar, Mike Neal, Tim Nedin, "T" Nickerson, Lynn Orkin, Martin Oroszco, Adam Perlman, Bill Picketts, Tom Price, David & Dana Pump, Leo Ramirez, Dr. Ken Ravizza, Emily Reaves, Steve & Teri Reed, The Roots, Pierre "Pooooch" Rudnunsky, David Samryeh, Kyle Sarosi, Steve Savage, Renee Scheer, John Schiffner (CCG), Dr. Mark Schoen, Al Schoenberger, Marc "Sirn" Schwartz, Bill Shaw, Mackie Shilstone, Dan Smith, John Snyder, Hal Stanton, Lisa Steinhart, The Stellos, Louis Suarez, Bob Tampkin, Dave Taylor, Jim Telgheder, Arn Tellem, Rick Thurman, The Troys, Doug Turner, Ron Twersky, University of San Francisco (1993), Dale Upshaw, Anthony Vallone, Jennifer Vides, Brian Vranesh, Rob Walley, Steve Wapnick, Paul Weisman, West Coast Baseball School, Matt Whisenant, Craig "Whit" Whitacre, Lance Whitaker, The Wilcox Family, Tim Worrel, Mieke Wouters, William Yanes, The Center for Yoga (Los Angeles) and Mike Zambri.

CONTENTS

*It's not about conquering the game
but allowing the game to play us
So stop trying to force effort
and climb aboard your raft
For the river flows spontaneously
along its uninhibited path*

A WORD FROM THE AUTHOR

Practice makes perfect, or so it is said, but are today's Western athletes practicing the right thing?

At the 1976 summer Olympics, the Soviet Union won more gold medals than any other country, including two of three judo events that were typically dominated by the Japanese. East Germany finished second overall, winning an unprecedented eleven of thirteen medals in women's swimming events.

Never before had any region of the world displayed such a dramatic rise in overall performance in such a short span of time. So astonished was the rest of the world that people began to suspect that the Soviet bloc countries were "doctoring" their athletes.

The truth of the matter is that the Soviets and their East German counterparts did not need to look to synthetic drugs or artificial stimulants for their sudden success. Ironically, in this era of scientific advancement, they looked to the traditional past.

By studying the highly developed minds of the Yogis, Martial Artists, and Zen Masters of China, Japan, and India, the Soviets devised and instituted mental training techniques that enabled their athletes to perform *under the most pressure-filled conditions* with a clear, calm and controlled mind.

Although today's Western athletes and their coaches are aware of the importance of being mentally prepared, they have failed to act upon it. This in spite of the fact that most players and coaches agree that winning and losing starts from "the shoulders up," that once competition begins, the game is *purely mental.* Yet most Western athletes still spend the majority of their time perfecting their *physical* skills, when it is the mental side of the game that ultimately determines who will succeed and who will fail.

When athletes are asked why they fail, they are likely to blame a mechanical flaw, or a physical shortcoming. But if pressed further, most athletes will admit that they fail because at some point prior to their performance, or at the moment of truth, "when it counts," they lose their confidence, their concentration, their composure.

In short, they lose their mental focus.

If athletes are going to be successful, they must be able to enter into a state of mind that allows them to unleash their talents without external distractions or internal inhibitions. In short, they must be able to perform **Un**-consciously.

Which brings us to the theme of this book.

Even though Western athletes have taken the necessary steps to prepare themselves physically, they have not yet begun to harness their greatest resource of all...their mind.

Most athletes will do whatever it takes to prepare themselves *physically* for their sport. They will run, stretch, lift weights, and practice their mechanics over and over. Because their bodies are in shape and they have put in long hours working on their skills, they believe they are completely prepared. But what have they done to prepare themselves mentally? What good is all their physical preparation, if their mind disrupts the execution of their physical performance? What good is physical preparation if the mind is not reliable or accountable during their performance? What good is physical preparation if their mind is an antagonist, rather than an ally?

Until athletes come to the understanding that they must cultivate their **minds** as they cultivate their **bodies**, they will continue to practice those areas of their game that are already spoken for. They will continue be at the mercy of mind-games, self defeating thoughts, distractions and mental blocks. They will continue to be limited as athletes.

Although it is accepted, even applauded for athletes to hire physical trainers, the misconception still persists that mental training is for "problematic" athletes. This is one misconception I hope to dispel with this book. The reality is that physical trainers and mental trainers have the same goal: to address current weaknesses (correction), to develop or sharpen skills (enhancement), and to neutralize potential obstacles (prevention).

This book is *not* written for problematic athletes, but for all athletes. It is for the successful athlete who wants to remain successful, the "can't miss" prospect who doesn't want to miss, the young player on his way up, the seasoned veteran player who wants to stay on top, the player who is streaking, and the player who is slumping. It is for the .260 hitter who wants to hit .300 and the bogey golfer who wants to close in on the 70s. It is for the amateur and the professional. It is for every athlete who wants to perform up to his or her[1] potential on a consistent basis.

Getting Focused, Staying Focused will show you how to use your mind to your *advantage*, not to your *disadvantage*; how to access your natural resources, at will.

By getting focused and staying focused, you will ensure that your "potential" is not just a label—that your mind is an **avenue**, and not an obstacle to realizing your potential.

---

1 The pronouns "he" and "his" are used in this book only for convenience, and also imply the feminine gender.

CHAPTER I

Identifying the Problem

Success is based upon the athlete's ability to trust his instincts. Failure occurs when this trust is questioned by the athlete's thoughts.

Can you imagine what would happen if a musician had to think between notes, a dancer between steps, a pitcher in the middle of his wind-up or a golfer in the middle of his back swing?

As athletes we've all heard phrases like, "you can't think and perform at the same time," "just let it happen," and "go with the flow." These are all ways of saying that athletes perform best when they perform in the *absence* of thought, or *Un*-consciously.

Just as a musician flows with the music or a dancer with the steps, our goal as athletes is to flow with the game—to allow our instincts to take over so that we can perform spontaneously. Yet, too often this doesn't happen. Too often Western athletes find that their thoughts interfere with their reactions, that their conscious thinking sabotages their instincts, that their performance is studied, contrived and mechanical.

This is not true of Eastern athletes.

If you've ever seen the performance of a Martial Artist, the Chinese acrobats, or a Zen Master, you have witnessed the perfect blend of the grace and balance of a ballerina with the concentration and precision of a surgeon. Eastern athletes, brought up in a culture that values instincts and downplays thinking, have learned to perform without the interference of conscious thought. Their performance is nothing more than an avenue to express their *natural* being, and thus their performance is fluid and spontaneous.

It seems clear that there *is* a difference between the Eastern athlete's performance and the Western athlete's performance. In order to understand this difference, we need to examine the differences between these two cultures.

THE ROLE OF THE ENVIRONMENT

When you walk into a dentist's office, you probably experience feelings of fear and apprehension. You've been hurt here before and you *expect* to be hurt again. This expectation is what is known in Psychology as a conditioned or *learned* response.

It was Ivan Pavlov, a Russian physicist and winner of the Nobel Prize in 1904, who proved that learned responses could be involuntarily induced by associating a specific stimulus with repeated reinforcements. In Pavlov's most famous experiment, he sounded a bell just prior to blowing food powder into the mouth of a dog. After a few days of the association of the bell ringing with the introduction of the food powder, the dog began to salivate *when he heard the bell ring* even in the absence of the food powder. Thus, it was proven that a conditioned stimulus (the bell) could produce an unconditioned response (salivation).

Although the intelligence of human beings and dogs can't be compared, the conditioning of learned behavior can. While we have not been conditioned by the sound of a laboratory bell, we have been conditioned by everything we have seen and heard all of our lives. We have been conditioned by our parents, teachers, peers, church, government, newspapers, billboards, magazines, radio and television.

We have all *learned* to act and react in certain ways due to the influences and expectations placed upon us by "society." These influences and expectations start from the time we are born, when girls are wrapped in pink blankets, and boys in blue. And whether we are *consciously* aware of it or not, society rings our bell every day.

So what does this have to do with *getting focused?*

Let's take a look at some of the *specific* differences between the East and West as they apply to athletes. In this way, we will see that an athlete's performance is nothing more than an extension of his or her culture, a reflection of his or her way of life.

EAST VS WEST

Throughout this book, I will be making comparisons between the cultures of the East and West. It is not my intention to glorify the East or belittle the West, but only to find what we can learn, and unlearn from each. The goal here is not one of separation, but of harmony—to understand and contrast these two different ways of life, in order to benefit our own life.

SOCIAL CONDITIONING—IMAGE VS. SUBSTANCE

The measure of success in today's Western society seems to be connected to money. It's important to have a nice car, beautiful furniture, stylish clothes, expensive jewelry, a top of the line stereo, television, VCR, camrecorder, and on and on. Our feeling of self-worth seems to be determined by how well we "display" our *exterior* self... our image. This pressure to acquire material possessions and the prestige that is associated with it has produced a society filled with competition and stress.

By contrast, Easterners are less concerned with material wealth and more concerned with spiritual growth. Therefore, the emphasis in the East is not on acquiring material wealth, but on developing one's *inner* self. Because material wealth creates an artificial image that lacks genuine substance, "toys" are often seen as an obstacle to spritual growth. Thus, it might be said of the East "that the one with the most toys loses."

"IDLE HANDS ARE THE DEVIL'S TOOL"

The Westerner is always in a hurry. We have so many obligations, places to go, people to see, things to do, that there's scarcely a minute in our day when we can take time to just sit and do nothing. What is worse, we probably don't want to "just sit and do nothing." We're so accustomed to keeping busy that if we do have a spare moment, we search for something to fill it with. We *need* to be busy or we feel guilty. And the busier we become, the more pressure we feel. There is never enough time to do all we think we should be doing, and consequently we live in a continual state of anxiety—even when we think we are relaxed.

Since Easterners are concerned with spiritual matters and the cultivation of their inner self, students of Eastern philosophy spend much of their time in solitude, contemplation and meditation. They are not under any pressure to go places or get things done. They are getting the most done when they attend to their inner growth.

Thus, without the pressure of time, or the need to be in two places at once, Easterners experience less anxiety and stress. They can take the time to realize the moment, and when in the moment, there is nothing but time.

TRUST IN OUR REASON, NOT IN OUR INSTINCTS

Albert Einstein, one of the greatest intellects of the 20th century said, "We should take care not to make the intellect our God. It has of course powerful muscles, but no personality."

We in the West have given complete authority to our thought processes. We have been taught to rely on our ability to *reason*. We have been taught that there is a *logical* answer for everything. That if we think long enough and hard enough we *will* find a solution. We've been told time and time again to "think before we speak," "look before we leap," "what is done in haste will be repented in waste."

Thus, we have been shaped to be *thinkers*, not *feelers*. We have been taught to trust our thinking, causing us to downplay our instincts. And even though our goal as athletes is to perform naturally, without thinking, we are afraid to do so. We are afraid to let go of the authority of our thoughts; afraid that our instincts will let us down; afraid that if we aren't thinking, we will lose control of ourselves and ultimately fail.

In the East, thoughts are viewed as deceptive tricks of the ego, temporary mental constructions that are subordinate to our intuitive feelings and instincts. Thus, Easterners trust their intuition more than they trust their intellect. To an Easterner,

The mind that thinks is one step behind.
The mind that acts is one step ahead.

CONGESTION VS. CLARITY

As a result of living in a materialistic, fast-paced, thought-oriented society, Westerners have become the victims of what I refer to as Mental Congestion.

Mental congestion is the complete saturation of our minds with thoughts. It is the result of *overthinking, stress and "sight and sound pollution."*

Overthinking occurs because we have been taught to trust our reason.

Stress occurs because we are always under pressure to succeed, to please others and live up to expectations.

Sight and sound pollution is the accumulation of everything we have ever seen or heard from the time we were born. For example, studies conducted by socioligists show that the average American is subjected to *several hundred* messages a day. And even though our minds are already on overload, the sights and sounds keep coming.

The result of Mental Congestion is a non-stop dialogue in our head. Even when we *don't want to think*, even when we *don't want to listen*, the thoughts continue. As athletes, we can all relate to this unwanted "chatter." It is there when we are trying to sink a two-foot putt, when we are about to make a free throw, when we are up at bat in the bottom of the ninth with the game on the line.

Not only does mental congestion undermine our confidence, but it has buried our natural instincts and destroyed our spontaneity. How can we perform spontaneously when we are constantly barraged by "thoughts"? Put rather simply,

> *If we are thinking, we can't possibly be reacting.*
> *If we are reacting, we can't possibly be thinking.*

Unfortunately, we in the West don't know how to turn off our thoughts, even if we want to. We don't have the tools to silence the constant chatter within us. With our brain constantly making comments and telling us what to do, is it any wonder we are unable to maintain our focus?

In the East, by comparison, the emphasis is on keeping the mind clear. The Easterner believes that the mind functions best when it is calm, and that our natural instincts emerge best when all thoughts cease to exist. Therefore, Easterners strive for clarity at all times, *especially* when performing.

THE SPLIT MIND OF THE WEST; THE UNIFIED MIND OF THE EAST

The philosophy of the East teaches us that we come into the world with a clear, uncluttered mind, a mind that is devoid of all thought, a mind that is pure feeling. This is what is called the "Unconscious" or the "original mind." It is the Easterner's belief that just as thin air cannot be split, the nature of one's mind cannot be split, for the mind is

Like a sword that cuts, but cannot cut itself;
Like an eye that sees, but cannot see itself.

In the West, however, through the "education" of society, we have developed a separate entity called "the ego." The ego is a manifestation of our intellect, an intellect that wants material comforts and possessions, that needs acclaim, wealth and social status. The result is that our intellect (ego) and intuition (feelings) seem to be in conflict, both vying for our attention. Thoughts seem to distract actions and actions seem to counter thoughts. The result of this tug of war is a "split" mind: the intellect standing aside to *ponder action* (contrivance); the *intuition* urging us to *leap into action* (spontaneity).

Since the Easterner is concerned with the cultivation of his *original mind* (Unconscious), and not his *"learned self"* (ego), he discounts his intellect and listens to his feelings. He believes the intellect is nothing more than a "collection" of thoughts, and that the true artist or athlete must be able to see through these temporary mental constructions and put his trust in the oneness of the original mind (Unconscious).

For a man rings like a cracked bell when he thinks and acts with a split mind—the intuitive or instinctive part wanting to leap into action, the intellect standing aside to interfere, control, condemn or admire.

In the East, the concept of the ego is seen as an illusion. Because this grasping self alienates us from our original mind (Unconscious), it is seen as an obstacle to spontaneous action. And since spontaneous action is the goal, one must "let go" of the ego in order to "free up" the mind and "leap into action."

For the Easterner, the consequences of living in an ego-less, intuitive environment have led to the perpetual cultivation of his or her natural mental resources. Thoughts are subordinate to feelings. The intellect and its resulting ego are shunned because they conflict with the harmonious nature of the original mind. This trust in one's original mind eliminates the confusion brought on by the over-abundance of thoughts, and prevents congestion from mounting in the first place.

This doesn't mean that all thoughts are destructive. Rather, one must contemplate the origin of a particular thought or thought pattern, identifying it as either a superficial voice of the ego (conditioning), or the affirmation of the intuition (original mind).

Free Will

Although we in the West have been programmed by the "laws of our own jungle," we are not condemned to go through life as Pavlov's dog. We are human beings, and as human beings we have the ability to identify and overcome the negative influences of our society. Remember,

Though the clouds may appear
to hide the sun
Behind the clouds
the sun is always shining.
Behind the mental congestion
the mind is always pure.

CHAPTER 2

Locating Our Resources: the Unconscious

Our Unconscious, or "original mind," is the source of all our talents and abilities. But before we can access these talents and abilities, we must be able to pierce the veil of mental congestion. To do this, we must first understand the two functions of the brain.

THE ROLE OF THE TWO HEMISPHERES OF THE BRAIN

"We can define a glass of water, but it will not quench our thirst."

—ALAN WATTS

Studies conducted by physiologists support the theory that the two hemispheres of the brain have two distinct characteristics.

The left hemisphere of the brain is the home of our language processing system: the database for all rational, logical and analytical skills. All thoughts that surface *consciously* we process and channel via the left hemisphere of the brain.

In sharp contrast to this, the right hemisphere of the brain is the conduit of our intuitive and instinctive feelings, our artistic, creative and athletic talents. All involuntary actions that occur spontaneously and *Unconsciously* are processed and channeled via the right hemisphere of the brain.

The left hemisphere of the brain communicates to us in words and we can access information from it on a conscious level. Therefore, we have developed a sense of *security* with the left hemisphere of the brain, even though our thoughts may be misguided, detrimental or self-defeating.

The right hemisphere of the brain cannot communicate with us in words. It can only communicate with us through pictures or feelings, and its information cannot be consciously retrieved—it can only be *revealed*. Therefore, we have developed a sense of *insecurity* with the right hemisphere of the brain.

The irony of this is that most athletes do *not* want to think while they are performing. They do not want their brain telling them what to do every time they are about to field a ground ball, shoot a free throw, or sink a putt. They realize that it is their thoughts that get them into trouble. And yet they continue to think their way through a performance.

So why do we give in to the authority of our thoughts?

There is a logical answer. Westerners, brought up in a "thought" oriented society, have *learned* to trust their intellect (left hemisphere), and distrust their feelings. Easterners, by comparison, are brought up in a society that is centered on creativity, spontaneity, and intuitiveness. They have learned to trust their feelings (right hemisphere), and distrust their thoughts.

THE TELEPHONE ANALOGY

If our thoughts are so detrimental to our performance then why don't we simply turn them off?

The answer is rather simple: we haven't learned how.

The left side of our brain is like a telephone that has a direct line of communication with us. Not only can we call it, but it can call us, and unfortunately, we don't even have to pick up the phone. This means that even when we choose *not* to listen, even when we don't *want* to listen, it continues spewing out its endless messages. These messages can be helpful. But they can also be harmful—especially in the case of athletes. They can undermine our confidence. They can fill us with self-doubts, fears and insecurities.

It is this "thinking" of the left side of our brain that interrupts the natural flow of our actions, that leads to paralysis through analysis, indecision instead of reaction. If we are to perform spontaneously, then we must learn to silence the chatter of the *left* side of our brain. We must learn to tap into the *right* side of the brain and the power behind it: the Unconscious.

THE POWER OF THE UNCONSCIOUS

Although miracles would not be accepted as a Western phenomenon, any scientist of merit would agree that the human brain, and the "mind" which transcends it, is itself a miracle.

Most of us have had unique or unusual experiences that seem unexplainable: deja vu, dreams, our sixth sense, and our flight or fight response. These are all phenomena that cannot be explained by empirical facts, and yet we know they exist. We have all encountered them.

Where do these "psychic" phenomena originate?

We know a great deal about the brain. We understand its control centers, its functions, its relationship to other parts of the anatomy. We understand that the brain can be predicted to do certain things, act certain ways, respond to specific chemicals or drugs. But we still don't understand and may never understand where the life force or "watchful eye of the mind" behind the brain comes from.

Thus, we may never be able to explain, empirically, the origin of psychic phenomena, but we do know that these experiences are driven by a force that is outside of conscious perception. This is what we refer to as the "mind" or the "Unconscious."

Where the West has tried to define the mind, the East accepts that some things are indefinable. Like the changing of seasons or a shooting star, the East recognizes that the mind is a force beyond our comprehension, beyond category, beyond definition. A force that works best when left alone.

What is the Unconscious?

"To bridge the gap between second-hand knowledge and first hand experience, we must call into play a higher faculty of mind known as the Unconscious. It is the 'Eye of the Spirit.'"

—Carl Jung

Trying to define the Unconscious is like trying to explain the unexplainable.

The dictionary defines it as a state unaccompanied by conscious experience; a state not known or apprehended to consciousness; a force that cannot be actively retrieved, rather a force that must be revealed on its own.

Although there have been many attempts to unveil its mysterious reality, the Unconscious may never be truly understood. Psychiatrists, psychologists and philosophers, however, have brought us valuable knowledge and insight into this universal force that exists in all human beings, so that we can identify specific characteristics associated with it.

The Unconscious is the source of all our natural abilities and resources. It is the source of our instincts and our reactions. It is a constant watchful eye that sharpens our senses in times of danger. It is always one step ahead of us. It is the knower and the known; the observer and the observed. It holds all fifty-two cards in the deck.

THE UNCONSCIOUS AND THE EAST

Because the word Unconscious, in literal translation, means to be unawake or unaware, Westerners have a hard time grasping its Eastern meaning. Although the East would agree that the Unconscious is a state unaccompanied by conscious experience, the **Eastern Unconscious** actually represents the highest state of *consciousness*. This is not in the sense of us making conscious or contrived decisions, but in the sense that spontaneous or intuitive decisions make us.

Ultimately, to be the best athletes we can be, we have to not only understand the role of the Unconscious, but to learn how to put it into action. Better yet, to learn how to let *it* put us into action.

THE UNCONSCIOUS AND GETTING FOCUSED

Sigmund Freud's most famous pupil, Carl Jung, believed that the Unconscious is the depository of all our wisdom, intuition, and instinctive abilities. If this is true, then wouldn't it be wonderful if we, as athletes, could tap into this source at will and use it to our benefit? In this book, we will learn how to do just that, how to bring the Unconscious into "conscious" awareness.

LOCATING THE UNCONSCIOUS

"An old man went looking frantically for his glasses, when all the while they were sitting on his nose."

—ZEN SAYING

Although we know very little about the Unconscious, the one thing we do know is that it surfaces in the absence of thought. In other words, it emerges without the methodical processing of the left hemisphere of the brain. It *is* a right brain phenomenon.

Since the Unconscious channels itself through the right hemisphere of the brain, it would follow that the right hemisphere of the brain is the avenue through which we can channel *all* of our natural resources.

THE UNCONSCIOUS AND THE ATHLETE

"In the case of archery, the archer ceases to be conscious of himself as the one who is engaged in hitting the bull's-eye which confronts him. This state of Unconsciousness is realized only when, completely empty and rid of the self (thought), he becomes one with perfecting the technical skill, which cannot be attained by any progressive study of the art."

—EUGEN HERRIGEL

All athletes have experienced it. The feeling of being "in the groove" or "on a roll." These are sporadic moments when everything seems to fall into place without conscious effort. At these moments, we feel that we can do no wrong. We are not aware of anyone else, and hardly aware of ourselves. We feel a physical and spiritual harmony between our body and our mind. We are having a *peak experience*.

This is the ultimate state of mind for every athlete. It is the feeling of the Unconscious taking over.

PLAYING UNCONSCIOUSLY—MAKING THE RIGHT CONNECTION

Just as the eyes will see and the ears will hear all by themselves, instincts and reactions will take over in the absence of conscious thought.

Renowned Zen master D.T. Suzuki once said, "If one really wishes to be a master of an art, technical knowledge alone is not enough. One must transcend technique so that the art becomes an 'artless art' growing out of the Unconscious."

What Suzuki is suggesting is that technical or theoretical knowledge can only teach you the process. Ultimately, you must trust a source that does not depend on orders or instructions, a source that transcends technical knowledge: your Unconscious.

When we are playing at our best, we are playing Unconsciously. Our Unconscious (right hemisphere) is in charge—and as long as we go with it—we will continue to perform at or near a peak level. But if we allow the thoughts of the left hemisphere of the brain to take over, we will have disrupted our flow; we will be mechanical (rigid), rather than natural (instinctive); we will be *conscious* rather than *Unconscious*.

CHAPTER 3

Mastering Yourself

If a man wants to be of the greatest possible value to his fellow-creatures, let him begin the long, solitary task of perfecting himself.

Many Westerners view life as something to conquer. Since life seems to be a series of problems, the average Westerner tries to put himself in a position to control all of the circumstances around him. If he loses control, he becomes frustrated.

The Easterner accepts that much that happens in life is out of his control. Like the waves in the ocean or the clouds in the sky, one's life is predictably unpredictable. To try to control all of the many variables that present themselves is like trying to hold water in the palm of your hands—no matter how hard you try, the water cannot be retained.

But the Easterner believes there is one variable in your life that you can control, and that is yourself. *You* are the one constant that ever was, is, or will be.

Mastering Yourself is learning how to take control of your life. It is learning how to channel your energy into yourself so that you can deal with whatever life sends your way. It is learning to look inward, not outward, for meaning, acceptance, and growth. It is learning to accept those circumstances you can't change, and change those circumstances you can.

Outside-In vs. Inside-Out

Because we are the product of Western society, we have been taught to look *outward* for approval and recognition. Our self-worth has been determined by the judgments or opinions of others. The car we buy, the clothes we wear, even our personalities are influenced by the pressures of society. Some of us may live our *entire* lives trying to please everyone but ourself.

I call this phenomenon "Outside-In." *Outside-In means that we are more concerned with how others view us than we are about how we view ourselves.*

Contrary to this, Easterners are not so concerned with "what others think." Easterners believe that one does not find self-worth in the approval of others, but from cultivating and nourishing one's inner self. This is what is called Inside-out. *Inside-out means that we are more concerned with how we feel about ourselves than what the world thinks of us.*

Because the Easterner looks *inward* to Master himself, he is rarely distracted by external factors. As a result his mind stays clear and focused.

Because the Westerner looks *outward* for approval, he is usually distracted by external factors and his mind becomes congested and unfocused.

This isn't to suggest that Easterners are numb to the external influences around them. Ironically, awareness is a basic characteristic among Easterners. But the opinions and judgments of others are observed rather than taken as the ultimate truth. For *truth* is something that must be revealed from within.

LOCATING TRUTH

We carry within us, the wonders we seek without us.

—SIR THOMAS BROWNE

Each of us carries within us a "sense of knowing" which I call "truth." Truth is a feeling that cannot be taught, but is the result of all our knowledge, experience, insight and intuition. It is our gut feeling, our hunch. It is that strong impulse that tells us what we already know.

In order to master ourselves, we must be able to look inward, to find the truth that is there, and to stay with that truth in spite of what may be happening around us.

Once we have come in touch with "truth" through, among other things, introspection, discipline and responsibility, we will no longer need to look outward for approval. We will learn to trust ourselves, to put stock in our own feelings despite the constant barrage of opinions and suggestions around us. We will have an inner understanding that will put all of the illusions, delusions, and deceptions of society behind us. We will no longer allow society to dictate who we *should* be, or what we *should* want. We will no longer need to look to others for answers, for we will know that most of our answers are found within ourselves.

A-Z: GIVING CREDIT WHERE CREDIT IS DUE

"If you don't get it from yourself, where will you go for it?"

—ALAN WATTS

Most of us do not take the time to give ourselves the credit that we deserve.

When was the last time you paid yourself a compliment? Conversely, when was the last time you paid a compliment to a friend, family member or fellow player?

Most of us are quick to see the good qualities in others, but are often harsh, critical and unforgiving of ourselves.

As we embark on the process of mastering ourselves, let us begin by giving credit where credit is due. Most of us have more wonderful qualities than we have ever taken the time to notice. Through the following exercise, we *will* take the time to discover or rediscover these qualities.

On a sheet of paper, list the letters A through Z. Next to each letter put down at least two words that describe a *positive* quality about yourself.

You can choose a quality that describes you as an athlete (enthusiastic, dedicated, durable), or it can be a quality that describes your general personality (honest, caring, dependable). These are not the qualities you wish you had, but a truthful evaluation of the qualities you do have.

It's important to be honest and objective. Crediting yourself with attributes you don't have in order to build a better image of yourself is only kidding yourself and counter-productive.

The point of the A to Z exercise is to give recognition to all the good things about yourself that you tend to overlook, to become aware of the positive attributes that genuinely and objectively reflect the person you are, and to give your spirit some well deserved nourishment.

Identifying these attributes is the first step towards discovering your true self, and discovering your true self is a necessary part of getting focused.

ELIMINATING DISTRACTIONS

The only time you see obstacles is when you take your eyes off your focus.

In the following section, we will take a look at the three distractions that most often divert our attention *away* from ourselves: external circumstances, trying to live up to the expectations of others, and competition.

I. External circumstances

Situations and Circumstances will come and go, but the flesh and bones will always remain.

Imagine that you are standing in the center of a merry-go-round. As long as you stay focused on the ground beneath your feet, you will always know where you are. But the moment your attention shifts to the horses on the periphery, your balance will be lost and you will find yourself at the mercy of the motion of the horses.

Too many athletes spend too much energy worrying about such circumstances as the weather, the fans, the media, the opponent, or the arena where they are performing. Since there is nothing we can do about these factors, it is best to "let them go." The more we dwell on them, the more we take the focus off ourselves.

You must begin to realize that regardless of who's in the stands, whether we're playing at home or on the road, whether it's rainy or sunny, as long as *we* remain constant, external factors cannot affect us. Circumstances may change, but our focus must never change.

II. Living up to the Expectations of Others

If you care about people's approval, you will become their prisoner.

—TAO TE CHING
(AS ADAPTED BY STEPHEN MITCHELL)

All of us want to do well, not just for ourselves, but to impress others. But if we are putting our focus into doing well for others, we have taken the focus off ourselves. Trying to impress "people that matter," and even those that don't matter, causes our minds to divide: half of our concentration on our performance, the other half in the stands.

If you are constantly worrying about succeeding for family, friends, coaches, scouts, and the public at large, then you cannot be focused on the game at hand. This isn't to suggest that it is wrong to "want" to do well in front of others, but doing well in front of others must be a *by-product* of doing well for yourself.

If we are to Master ourselves, then we must get past this desire to impress others.

III. Competition

Mastering others is temporary. Mastering ourselves is permanent.

Although the Westerner has grown accustomed to thinking of "competition" as healthy and necessary, the Easterner looks on it as negative and destructive. Since the opponent is always changing and unpredictable, spending time worrying about the opponent is a waste of time. To an Easterner it is the *self*, and not the *opponent*, who must be won over.

COMPETITION AND THE WEST: DEFEATING THE OPPONENT

The Easterner's view of competition may be difficult for the Westerner to understand, for competition has always been an integral part of our political, economic, educational and social structure.

We have been taught from an early age, the "importance" of "outdoing" our peers. In school, we are judged not on our own merit, but how well we measure up *against* our school-mates. Thus, even if we are doing the best we can, we may feel like failures. This attitude follows us into the work place, where again we are pitted one against the other. Instead of working in harmony with our fellow employees, we are often trying to outdo them.

This "survival of the fittest" mentality not only puts additional stress on us, but in turn widens the gap between us and our fellow human beings. Thus, competition leaves us sparkling on the outside, but hollow on the inside.

Athletes have been particularly vulnerable to the *negative* effects of competition. For example, most of us think that a rival opponent will get us "fired up" or motivate us to play at a higher level. But the truth is that this short term motivation leads to a long term detrimental result. Because competition takes the focus away from ourselves, it also creates a division in our attention: part of us thinking about our performance, part of us worried about our opponent's performance.

For those of you who make it a habit of looking over your shoulder, or worrying about the competition, you have fallen victim to the trap of the Western mentality. You have failed to realize that if your game is fully polished and fined-tuned, you don't need to worry about what the competition is doing.

The truth is, once you have mastered yourself, your opponent is already mastered.

COMPETITION AND THE EAST: HARMONY

Contrary to the competitive ways of the West, Eastern philosophy does not see life as one individual trying to outdo the other, but as a coming together of all individuals for the good of the whole.

In contrast to Western individualism, the East believes that there is a common bond, a universal source that links all human beings.

Thus, competition is seen as a barrier to universal advancement, an obstruction to a mind whose inherent nature is harmonious with all beings. The sun does not choose to shine on one individual in the midst of others, and if nature treats all human beings equally, then who are we to separate and divide? Since the Easterner is more concerned with the good of the whole, he is not likely to be selfish or egocentric. Thus, *contribution* replaces *consumption, cooperation* replaces *competition* and people are seen as allies, not enemies.

This harmony is not just a surface kindness, but a deep bond between people, a bond created by the nature of giving. When one gives, one is not only nurturing the receiver, but nurturing oneself. Ironically, the good feelings generated by helping another are usually greater for the giver than the receiver.

Thus, where a competitive lifestyle creates gaps, a harmonious lifestyle closes gaps. Where "taking" makes you feel rich in status, "giving" makes you feel rich in spirit. And it is this connection to our spirit that enhances both our personal life and our sport.

Winning Over Yourself: A Case of Aikido

Aikido is a Japanese martial art based on an ancient form of self-defense. Aikido's emphasis is to bring all situations back into harmony; to learn how to *redirect* the opponent's energy, rather than attempt to match power with power. It was founded by Professor Morihei Uyeshiba (1883-1969) as a reaction to the *competitive* and combative nature of the martial arts.

Uyeshiba, a master of several martial arts and considered unbeatable with a sword, came to realize that true self defense is not winning over *others*, but winning over the discord *within yourself*. This is done by spending time mastering yourself; by learning how to get past your own restrictions, inhibitions and shortcomings; and by lifting the veil from within in order to unleash and tap into the unlimited abilities and talents that often lie dormant in our Unconscious.

The Aikidoist strives to maintain a stable balance by being in complete control of his mind and body. Through a calm and alert posture, Aikido movements employ the fundamental dynamics of the entire person (physical, mental, spiritual). Learning how to unite these dynamics is what the Aikidoist calls *harmony*. And once the Aikidoist has created this balance, attention directed anywhere but inward will only disrupt this harmony.

MA: ELIMINATING THE OPPONENT

One of the most interesting aspects of Aikido is the notion of *Ma*. *Ma* will give you a better understanding of why the opponent is ultimately a distraction; why a "competitive" edge is not earned by focusing on your competition.

Let's examine the classic confrontation between pitcher and batter. Both are caught up in the *Ma* of trying to "outdo" the other. The pitcher is attempting to throw off the batter's timing, while the batter is trying to outwit or out-guess the pitcher. They have both *created Ma* because each one is trying to win over the other, forgetting about their *own* concentration and preparation.

If they would each put all of their focus on themselves, the pitcher concentrating on his target—the batter looking for his pitch to hit—then they will each have eliminated the *Ma*, enabling them to perform without the inhibition or anxiety that exists because the opponent exists. Like the accomplished Aikidoist, in order to get focused and stay focused, we must learn to win over ourselves; to *eliminate* the *Ma*. By eliminating the *Ma* we will overcome any doubts or desires that arise because an opponent exists. By keeping ourselves in harmony we will not dilute the precious energy that is lost when trying to combat an opponent.

LAYING DOWN OUR TRACKS

Once you have made the commitment to master yourself, you will be like a train traveling along a set of tracks.

By keeping the focus on yourself, you will move forward at a very steady and controlled rate of speed, unaffected by where you are, what kind of day it is, who is watching, or who your opponent is. Bounded and confined by each new portion of track, it will not be a question of "if" you will reach your destination, but "when" you will reach it.

CHAPTER 4

Meditation: An Inactive Clearing of the Mind

"In the pursuit of knowledge, every day something is added. In the practice of meditation, every day something is dropped."

—TAO TE CHING
(AS ADAPTED BY STEPHEN MITCHELL)

In this chapter, we will take the first step in getting focused: clearing our mind through meditation.

In the book's introduction we referred to the fact that the Soviets utilized the mental training techniques of the Yogis, Martial Artists and Zen Masters of the Far East to enhance the performance of their athletes.

Before implementing these techniques, however, the Soviets devised several studies to prove the effectiveness of the Easterner's mind control. Of these studies, none seemed to be more conclusive than the statistics taken from the meditative techniques of the Yogis. Specifically, the significant role that (diaphragmatic) breathing plays in both physical and *mental* well being.

Because the role of one's breath is fundamental to most meditative techniques, the Soviets were able to hone in on the connection between diaphragmatic breathing and favorable physiological changes in bodily functions.

Statistics confirmed that heightened states of mind, attained through concentration and breathing exercises, enabled the Yogis to control various physiological bodily functions. The most notable changes were an increase in Alpha Waves (brain waves associated with calmness and well being), and a marked decrease in the body's oxygen consumption or metabolism. Decreased oxygen consumption, or hypometabolism, is conducive to lower blood pressure, lower respiratory rate and lower levels of blood lactate (lactate is purported to be associated with anxiety).

All of these results suggested that through the control of certain *voluntary* acts, *involuntary* mechanisms in the body can be altered. One's breathing *can* affect one's "performance."

Though the Soviets were the first to apply these techniques to sports, the philosophy and purpose they serve date back some 3,000 years. Needless to say, mental "training" is nothing new. But applying it to *sports* in our day is.

The Stigma of Meditation

Perhaps because it originated in the Far East, the practice of meditation carries with it a certain stigma. Westerners, unfamiliar with Far Eastern culture, often associate it with "mystical," "supernatural," or "occult" experiences, and people who meditate are often viewed as odd or strange.

Americans are particularly skeptical. Perhaps because they have grown up in the most powerful nation in the world, and therefore believe that their culture is superior to any other. Unfortunately, this narrow-mindedness has closed the door on benefits we might derive from other cultures, one of which is meditation.

Meditation is not a religion or sect. It is not a rigid exercise that is restricted only to certain areas of our life, but a practice that affects and enriches every aspect of our existence. It is an art form, and like any art form, the more we work at it, the more rewarding it will be.

Meditation is an art, and as such it is unlimited and unlimiting.

Meditation Defined

"Meditation is the art of suspending verbal and analytical thinking for a time, somewhat as a courteous audience will stop talking when a concert is about to begin."

—Alan Watts

If you've ever been at a deserted beach, on a mountain top, camping or fishing in the great outdoors, then you have probably had a meditative experience. Believe it or not, most of us meditate on a daily basis without even realizing it.

By definition alone, you are meditating if, 1) you are in a quiet environment, 2) you are in a comfortable position, (3) your awareness is absorbed by the present moment, and (4) this awareness is directed by a continuous sight or sound.

For example, let's say that you are on vacation at a quiet beach resort. After dinner, you decide to go for a walk to catch the sunset. There is no one around, and it is unusually peaceful. You listen to the sound of the waves breaking against the shore, and watch the red hue of the sun descending below the horizon. As day drifts into night, a feeling of calm overtakes you. You are absorbed by the gentle breeze, the splash of the waves, the color of the sunset. Your mind empties and you feel at one with nature. You are meditating.

Athletes also experience the meditative state without realizing it. Let's say you are the pitcher in a baseball game. It's the fourth inning and you've retired the first nine batters in order. You begin to "sense" you are on a roll. Each pitch you throw seems to make a distinct sound as it pops into the catcher's glove. This distinct sound seems to pull the ball in all by itself. It's as if the ball knows exactly where it's going. Suddenly, both the strike zone and the catcher's glove seem twice as big. A quiet aura permeates your mind as everything else around you seems to fade out of sight. Without even trying, you can do no wrong. In theory, you are also meditating.

Let's examine how both examples fulfill the requirements of the four components of meditation:

• Obviously, in the first example, the environment was quiet. But it was also quiet on the pitcher's mound, for as any pitcher knows, once you have found your zone, you are basically unaware of your surroundings. Though there might be a great deal of noise in a ballpark, the pitcher who has found his rhythm could just as easily be on an isolated beach.

- As for the comfortable position, again, the beach is obviously a comfortable place, but for the pitcher, the playing field is equally comfortable. It is his home away from home.

- The person caught up in the beauty of the sunset and the pitcher concentrating on each pitch are both *in* the present moment.

- Finally, the sight of the sun setting and the continuous sound of the waves breaking on the shore fulfills the requirement of the repetition of sight and sound, as does the sight of the catcher's brown leather glove and the sound of the continuous popping of the pitches.

Although meditation consists of these four basic ingredients, the power of meditation cannot be reduced to mere definition. By entering a thought-less state of being, meditation cultivates and nourishes one's mind. Through meditation one finds peace, clarity and relaxation. Because of meditation, one gains control over his or her body and feels at one with nature.

THE PHILOSOPHY BEHIND MEDITATION

Original Mind

People often think that meditation is a practice that takes us to a place outside of our body, to a *special* state of mind. But the truth is meditation takes us "back" to our *original* state of mind. The key word here is "back," because we are not actually adding anything or going anywhere. Just as a sculptor reveals his image by removing pieces of stone, we too reveal our original mind and its resources by removing the veil of mental congestion.

The term "original mind" is borrowed from its Eastern origins where the mind is considered to be born in complete harmony with nature, free from the "education" (socialization/conditioning) of society. Eastern thought believes that the "education" of society is often harmful in that it fosters the growth of the ego rather than the spirit. The ego distorts our inherent *peace* of mind, creating a second mind or self that alienates us from the naturalness of our original mind. By removing the delusion of our "learned" self, meditation awakens us from our cultural trance (life's daily worries), silences the "educated" self (ego) and returns us back to the spontaneous nature of our original mind (spirit).

The Present Moment

To access our original mind, we must first learn how to quiet our active thoughts and bring our entire focus to the innocence of the *present* moment. When we have learned to silence all thoughts and are completely absorbed by the present moment, we may experience a vivid sensation known as an *awakening*. An awakening is the feeling that we have touched our very essence. When this happens, the world and all of its turbulence ceases to exist and we are at one with this essence. But this sensation will not come by trying to *acquire* it. It comes by itself, as a byproduct of meditation.

Letting Go

This brings us to another principle of meditation: letting go. Letting go means that we allow all thoughts to pass as they arise; to see things as they are without forming opinions or judgements; to achieve a state of quiet awareness, without comment. This state of awareness, like an awakening, cannot be acquired; rather, it reveals itself. By letting go we learn that we do not need to grasp or push things away. Whether it be thoughts, emotions or physical sensations, in time everything will just rise and pass naturally, without interference on our part. If one stops to grasp, accept, or even reject a passing thought, then one has become *attached* to that thought. Instead, we must view all thoughts as temporary, and allow them to pass without conscious intervention.

Neutrality

Allowing thoughts to pass without "attaching" to them is called *neutrality*. By remaining neutral, our clutter of thoughts will begin to dissipate. Because we are neither accepting nor rejecting thoughts, the interplay between our thoughts, on the one hand,

and our self, on the other, will be severed. But most important, our "self" will no longer play an active role in our thinking and our thoughts can be *observed* rather than judged.

In order to clear our mind, we must remain neutral. As a newcomer to meditation we may find it difficult not to respond or *participate* with our thoughts, but as our practice continues we will learn that thoughts will come and go on their own. Just as birds make their way across the horizon until they are no longer in sight, thoughts too will pass across our minds and disappear, if given a chance.

Diaphragmatic Breathing

Learning to breathe deeply and fluidly through your diaphragm is at the core of meditation.

Even though breathing through one's diaphragm is the *natural* way to breathe, most Americans do not breathe this way. Because Americans are always in a hurry, they do not take the time to let their breath descend into the cavity of their diaphragm, but instead take short, choppy breaths. This is known as chest breathing. Chest breathing is synonymous with "stressful" breathing, because not enough oxygen can reach the vital organs of the body, thereby causing the body to strain for its ample supply of air.

Oxygen also plays a vital role in circulation throughout the body, carrying nourishment and healing energy directly to each cell. Studies have repeatedly shown that heart rate, respiratory rate and blood pressure decrease significantly as a result of several forms of diaphragmatic breathing (i.e. Pranayama Yoga, Zazen and Transcendental Meditation).

In addition to the diaphragm being the center of breathing, in many Eastern philosophies the area just below the diaphragm is considered to be the center of the human spirit. According to Hindu and Buddhist yogic systems, there are a number of psychic centers in the body through which cosmic force or vital energy (Ki) flows. The *Hara*, or the lower abdominal region is one such center. Like the spokes of a wheel merging into their center (or hub), our psychic forces and bodily functions merge into each other in the body's center of gravity, the Hara. It is this region that is the link between body, mind and soul. (Of course, a Westerner may have difficulty accepting that his spirit resides in the center of his body, when his brain [or his intellect] is located at the top of his anatomy. But Easterners would remind us that thoughts are merely temporary mental constructions, not the essence of our being).

Diaphragmatic breathing allows us to connect to our Hara. It switches our focus from the top of our anatomy (intellect) to the center of our anatomy (intuition). It allows us to access the source of our Unconscious nature and *liberates* us from the stranglehold of our thoughts. This transition from the conscious to the Unconscious allows us to enter into an intimate relationship with our true nature. As our attachment is removed from our thoughts, the innocence and optimism of the present moment can finally be realized. And with this moment comes clarity, insight, wisdom and meaningfulness.

The Practice of Meditation

Setting the Stage

Before beginning the actual practice of meditation, there are certain steps that we can take to ensure the consistency and progress of our meditative experience. These have to do with *where* we meditate, *when* we meditate, our *posture*, our *clothing* and *preliminary deep breaths*. Let's examine each one of these.

Where

- **Choose a quiet place**

  If our goal is to quiet the mind, it is important to eliminate as many distractions as possible. Any quiet room in your home is suitable, but if the opportunity presents itself, try meditating outdoors. The beach, the mountains, even your own backyard tends to deepen and authenticate your experience.

- **Meditate in the same environment each day**

  By meditating in the same environment each day, your mind will begin to associate your place of practice with your purpose of practice. Just as the mere sight of free weights, nautilus machines, and Stairmasters will remind you that it's time to get into a workout frame of mind, the mere sight of your meditation environment will likewise alert and prepare your mind for its "workout."

- ## Hang your "do not disturb" sign on the door

  If you have a spouse, a roommate, or live with other family members, then it is important to inform them that you are designating a certain time and place to meditate and that you should not be disturbed. Unplug your phone or let your answering machine take your messages. Minimize as many potential distractions as possible so that your session will not be interrupted.

When

- ## Stipulate a set time each day

  Because we are creatures of habit, it is important to reserve the same time each day for your meditation.[1] As with the location, your mind will automatically adjust to a certain time as being the time to meditate. Also, you are most likely to stay with your meditation if it is part of your daily routine, instead of wondering when or if you will have time to fit it in. Each session should last approximately twenty minutes.

- ## Mornings are best

  Ideally, it's best to wake up thirty minutes earlier in the morning and take ten minutes to come fully awake before meditating. Also, by meditating in the morning, you will feel as if you are starting your day on a good note. But if mornings are not feasible, any time of day is acceptable as long as you make that time a *priority*.

---

1   Avoid meditating after heavy meals. The digestive system will be very active after a large meal, and this will make breathing out of the stomach a difficult task.

Posture

- **Choose a comfortable position**

  If you prefer to sit, I suggest a reclining chair indoors or a patio chair outdoors. If you decide to lie down, be sure that your head is elevated by placing a large pillow or cushion beneath your head. Although it is most beneficial (for reasons beyond the scope of this book) to have your spine at a ninety degree angle, in the early going it is more important to sacrifice a little bit of effectiveness for comfort.

  Even though you are technically relaxing while meditating, you must be sure that you are not susceptible to falling asleep (unless meditation is being used as an aid to insomnia).

Clothing

- **Wear clothes that are loose and comfortable**

  Sweat pants and cotton shirts are ideal, but anything that does not restrict the stomach from expanding is acceptable. Also, shoes and socks should be removed. Because your feet house an abundance of sensitive regions or "meridians," air can circulate more easily when your feet are exposed.

Preliminary Breathing

- **Take "warm-up" breaths**

  Once you are in your quiet place, at your set time, in a comfortable position, wearing comfortable clothing, begin to inhale and exhale several times through your nose. (If you have an obstructed nasal passage, you may breathe through your mouth). Soften your stomach and imagine that it is a large balloon. As you take in each inhalation, try to imagine that the balloon in your stomach is filling with air, and that your entire rib cage is expanding from the front and back. When the balloon is fully expanded, begin to exhale the air at a very slow and even pace.

After a few of these "warm up" breaths, you are now ready to begin the practice of meditation.

THE THREE STAGES OF MEDITATION

"Only until you have no-thing in your mind and no mind in things can you be vacant and spiritual, empty and marvelous."

—ALAN WATTS

As you may have noticed, meditation is often referred to as a "practice." This is because meditation is a continual process. It is never mastered; it is never finished.

Although there are many different schools of meditation, there is no right way to meditate. In this book, we will present three of the most common methods. They will be set forth in order of difficulty, and are designed to help you systematically gain control over your breath. Once your breath has been brought under control, your mind will follow. If practiced diligently and consistently, the first two exercises can be accomplished in a week's time. The third exercise has no time table, for it is this form of meditation that you will continue to practice for the rest of your life.

Remember that meditation is a practice in self-discipline, concentration and fortitude, so do not become discouraged if at first you find it difficult to remain quiet for even a few minutes. Because our minds are so accustomed to chatter and activity, we cannot expect to silence our thoughts in a single session. But in time, if we stick to our practice, we will learn that with *less* effort, the mind will harness itself.

Meditation is a skill, and like any skill, it will take time to perfect. But the very fact that you are embarking on this journey is symbolic of your will to grow and find greater meaning in life.

STAGE I: AWARENESS: LISTENING TO THE BREATH

Although this exercise many seem simple, there are several things that you will learn. For starters, you will see that you are breathing *incorrectly* (chances are that you are breathing through your chest). You will also notice how difficult it is to remain completely silent and focused on your breathing without the intrusion of thoughts. Finally, you will realize how active and prevalent your thoughts are, even when you are *trying* to ignore them.

EXERCISE #1:

Find a comfortable position, close your eyes and focus your attention on your breathing. Since you are going to try to breathe through your diaphragm, soften your stomach and imagine that your mind is located just below your navel. Listen only to your breath. See how long you can remain focused on your breath without the intrusion of thoughts. If your thoughts become too overwhelming (prevalent), open your eyes and start from the beginning.

STAGE II: COUNTING THE BREATH

During the previous exercise, you probably found that your thoughts were very active, making it difficult to maintain your focus on the inactivity of your breathing. For a beginner especially, keeping the mind clear amidst the constant chatter of our thoughts seems futile. That's why most beginning meditative techniques include some point of reference in conjunction with the inhaling and exhaling of air from the diaphragm. The repetition of a word like "peace," the counting of numbers, or the reciting of a phrase allows the practitioner to bind or fasten himself to a single focus. In effect, this point of reference supersedes all other thoughts and feelings. Distractions move to the periphery as the point of reference takes center stage.

In this exercise, instead of passively listening to your breath, you will begin to actively regulate it. You will do this by chronologically assigning numbers in conjunction with each phase of the breath.

Actively counting breaths, or the repetition of a word ("Mantra"), is like a bridge over troubled waters, a net beneath a high wire act. It gives us a sense of support, a rope or scaffold to hold onto until we are able to displace this activity with unconscious concentration.

EXERCISE #2:

Find a comfortable position and close your eyes. Again soften your stomach and bring your entire mind, your entire focus down to your diaphragm.

As you take in your first inhalation of air, say the number "one" to yourself throughout the duration of your breath. As your diaphragm fills up, hold onto the number one. Then, as you begin to exhale, say the number "two" to yourself. When this air exhausts, inhale again and say the number "three" to yourself. Continue in this manner all the way up to ten, then reverse the order back down to one again. If you are distracted at any point, start over and try again. In the early going, it may be a good idea to start with realistic goals like going from one to four and back, one to six and back, and so on. When you feel that you can consistently make it to ten and back without any conscious interference, then it is time to remove the training wheels and move on to the final stage.

STAGE III: TRANSCENDING THE BREATH

To transcend means to *go beyond* mechanical effort. Just as we all learned to tie our shoelaces mechanically before doing it "without thinking," we will now learn to follow our breath without being aware of it.

Where counting numbers eliminated the majority of our thoughts and distractions, it still involved some conscious intervention. Our goal now will be to remove *all* thoughts so we can follow our breath, and then transcend it so we can simply *be*.

Transcending the breath is a very advanced form of meditation and it should only be attempted with great patience and perseverance. When the support system of your numbers is gone, there will be nothing for you to hold onto...except *nothingness*. It is at this point that the mind will clear, the Unconscious will merge with the conscious, and all of life can be understood.

EXERCISE #3:

Find a comfortable position and close your eyes. Soften your stomach and bring your entire mind, your entire focus down to your diaphragm.

Acclimate yourself by taking some deep breaths. Become aware of just your breath and follow it for a minute or two. Imagine that nothing else exists in the entire Universe other than your breath. Turn all of your trust and faith over to your breathing. Then imagine that your breath is breathing you rather than you breathing it. You should no longer try to actively control the pace or structure of your breath. Just allow it to rise and fall on its own.

At this point, there is no longer a distinction between the breather and the breathing, the observer and the observed. You should feel that "I" no longer breathe the air; *it* breathes me. Your breath and you are, in fact, *one*.

As your mind begins to empty you will feel a sense of peace. Now simply allow the harmonic forces of your mind and body to take control. Once again, you no longer have to worry about effort, for just as the eyes are trusted to see and the ears are trusted to hear, the breath can now be trusted to breathe.

As all conscious effort ceases to exist, there is nothing left to do but trust your mind, let go of yourself and simply be.

A Final Word On Meditation

"Sitting Quietly, Doing Nothing
Spring Comes, and the Grass Grows by Itself."

It may seem both strange and unreasonable that strong and intelligent men and women should simply sit or lie still to improve their mental well being. But it should be remembered, that just as a glass of muddy water is best cleared by leaving it alone, mental congestion, stress and tension are best cleared through the inaction of meditation.

CHAPTER 5

Discipline:
An Active Clearing
of the Mind

Discipline provides us with the inspiration to take the right course of action, regardless of the pain or sacrifice involved.

In the last chapter we saw the role that meditation plays in removing mental congestion and calming the winds of discursive thinking. In the luxury of a quiet and comfortable environment, meditation allows you to clear the mind by using a passive or "inactive" approach.

However, we must take into account that the majority of our day does not offer us the luxury of a peaceful environment. In fact, most of our waking hours are spent in the turbulence of a stressful society, where the mind is over-active and vulnerable to counter-productive thinking.

If we are to truly clear the mind, we must be as aware of our "public" time as we are of our "private" time. We must understand that the same mental congestion that is being *passively* removed in our private time can quickly mount in the public sector.

Therefore, we need a reliable tool to *actively* clear our mind and keep it free from negative influences in our "public time."

Discipline is that tool.

Discipline will not only enable us to take control of the problems and distractions that arise on a daily basis, but to embark on new challenges with enthusiasm. It will strengthen our inner core as it leads us along the path of *Truth*.

THE TRUTH OF DISCIPLINE

Laziness satisfies our ego; Discipline satisfies our truth.

In the last chapter we discussed the meaning of truth. As you'll recall, truth is the sense of knowing that comes to us from our inner self. It is the voice of our *intuition*. It is the feeling that knows right from wrong on an Unconscious level.

But truth is often *not* the path of least resistance. In fact, truth often seeks the path of *more* resistance. By demanding that we confront problems, make sacrifices, and challenge old patterns of behavior, it often forces us into painful or uncomfortable positions.

Thus, a dilemma arises for the Westerner whose Unconscious is urging him to seek truth regardless of the consequences, but whose lazy tendencies are tempting him to take the easy way out.

DISCIPLINE AND GROWTH

Personal growth occurs when we begin confronting problems, rather than avoiding them.

Most people tend to seek pleasure and avoid pain. Theoretically, there is nothing wrong with this principle if we know our limitations. But when we avoid personal growth because it is "too painful," when we avoid our problems because "they" are too painful, when we avoid unpleasant situations that need to be faced because they are "too painful," then we have gone too far.

What we fail to realize is that the process of meeting and solving problems makes us stronger, more confident and more capable. It is for this reason that we should actually welcome problems rather than avoid them—to see them as opportunities to grow—to see them as building blocks of our character.

However, most of us will go to extraordinary lengths to avoid "the call" of discipline. In our effort to escape the least inconvenience, we will continue to hope that our problems will go away on their own. Yet the avoidance of problems ultimately becomes *more* painful than the problems themselves, for the Unconscious, which seeks the truth in all matters, won't allow us to rest until the job gets done.

The path of least resistance takes several forms. Three of these are *Laziness, Rationalization* and *Procrastination*. These are all devices of our left brain to ignore, delay, and avoid painful or unpleasant situations.

Laziness: The Antithesis of Discipline

Laziness is defined as "the failure to work, take responsibility, or extend oneself when confronting problems or issues." It is the antithesis of discipline.

Discipline is self-control; laziness is self-indulgence. Discipline is following truth at all costs; laziness is putting comfort ahead of truth. Discipline is confronting our problems; laziness is hiding from our problems. Discipline requires strength of character; laziness shows no character.

It is easy to see why Westerners are more *vulnerable* than *resistant* to laziness. Our culture seems focused on leisure, on making enough money so we can "sit back and relax." The work ethic has been replaced by the "play" ethic. And when we do work hard, it is usually to acquire more possessions or more free time.

As a result of this leisure-oriented mentality, many Westerners try to get away with doing as little as possible. We do not set difficult goals for ourselves, but tend to take the easy way out. We would rather watch television than read a book. We have forgotten that our reach should exceed our grasp.

Procrastination and Rationalization

Procrastination is the art of delaying what we know we should be doing until some later point, or indefinitely. We might procrastinate because we are lazy, because we don't want to face an unpleasant situation, or because we're afraid we may fail. In any case, the results are the same. The job may never get done.

Rationalization is the method our thoughts (left brain) use to *justify* our being lazy or procrastinating. It is these thoughts that make it "okay" if we don't adhere to truth; that make it okay to carry the burdens of jobs undone; that make it okay to avoid the pain, sacrifice or effort involved in meeting a task head on. It is rationalization that leads us to believe that all of our problems will go away.

The reality is that most issues, problems or confrontations do not go away. The reason they found their way into our life to begin with is that they need our attention and usually need it *now.* Laziness, Procrastination and Rationalization give us false hopes that the unavoidable can be avoided, that we can escape the inevitable.

In order to get focused and stay focused, we must overcome these three detrimental forces, and discipline is the way we will do it.

Getting Disciplined

Laziness, procrastination, and rationalization are "learned behaviors" and like other "learned behaviors," they can be "unlearned." The following exercises will enable us to win the battle of discipline over these three forces by learning how to identify truth, and then back it up with assertive action. Although discipline takes effort and the will to confront problems that may be difficult or painful, its rewards are plentiful. Not only will we remove the stress and congestion caused by problems, but we will gain an inner strength and a feeling of peace, knowing that the *right* action was taken rather than avoided. Once we realize our own power, we will begin to welcome those situations that once seemed insurmountable.

Making Black and White Decisions

Instead of worrying, doubting, questioning or pondering a difficult situation, try asking yourself this simple question: "What does my truth tell me about this situation?" In other words, without trying to analyze or reason, listen to your "gut feelings," your *intuition.*

If you find it difficult to differentiate between your "gut feelings" and your "cerebral thoughts," try putting yourself in a quiet environment, take a few deep breaths and allow your mind to quiet and still. What you'll discover is that the quieter your mind becomes, the clearer you can hear the unmistakable voice of your intuition.

Once the truth of your intuition is heard, do not judge or analyze it. Instead, trust it with all your heart and immediately "leap into action."

For an Easterner, to "leap into action" is to endorse one's inner truth with *spontaneous* action. In other words, don't spend time swaying between alternatives. Listen to your truth and move forward like a snowball rolling down a hill.

By taking this approach, your decisions will be black and white, and so will your actions. Consequently, there will be little or no room to question your actions, and you will be spared the second and third guessing that normally paralyzes us. In fact, you will have taken the wisest course of action. You will have looked beyond the consequences of the situation by adhering to the only condition that matters—Truth.

Making black and white decisions will get to the heart of the matter by seeing past the consequences of making the "right" or "wrong" decision. If you comply with your own truth, then you will always have made the "right" decision. Naturally, trusting your intuitive feelings without any conscious deliberation may take some practice, but as you begin to downplay the importance of your thoughts, your mind will become more sensitive to the advice that truth is giving you.

THRESHOLD: DIGGING DEEP BY CHALLENGING OLD TENDENCIES

Remember, truth will surface if given a chance, but also remember that our thoughts are very influential, persuasive and deceptive. Though it will be in our best interest to trust truth, our ego will make it difficult to "break the chain" of pleasure. Hence, we may find ourselves still going to extraordinary lengths to avoid the potential discomfort of disciplined actions.

But, if we are to gain back control over our mind, we must break this chain. We must see past the "tricks" and "deception" of the ego that may make us feel good for the time being, but which we will regret in the long run.

We can make this break by digging deep into our will and having the courage to challenge our "comfortable" tendencies. We must go beyond the conscious experience to access that place where truth resides and the destructive desires of the ego do not exist.

DISCIPLINE EXERCISES

The following two exercises will put you in touch with your truth by teaching you how to "hear" your intuition, and then act accordingly.

Each exercise should be maintained for a week. Once you make your commitment to follow through with these exercises to test your discipline and access your truth, you must take your commitment seriously. Either put something in writing or let someone know what you are doing, and give them your word that you will comply with your commitment. I've found that signing your name to a contract has a sense of legitimacy about it.

Either way, once you decide on your discipline exercises, you will realize that there is nothing to think about—there are no deals or compromises to make. The conditions of these exercises should be black and white. This will minimize potential obstacles that "convenient" thought patterns will throw your way.

EXERCISE 1: Doing what you should not be doing

Spend a few minutes thinking about your daily habits. Are there any major issues in your life that you need to confront? Are there any particular behaviors that are bothersome to you? Is there something about these behaviors that are clouding your focus, that conflict with truth?

Chances are that you, like everyone else, continue to do things on a daily basis that are counterproductive to your focus. It can be any number of things like oversleeping, eating too much, or biting your fingernails. Whatever the habit, we often find it difficult to summon the will power to change.

Discipline will *require* us to confront these issues. Pick a habit that is no longer conducive to your focus. Again, it is something that is present in your daily life that no longer agrees with truth. No matter what's at stake, no matter what the cost, make a commitment to yourself that you will no longer give in to this habit for the next week. At the onset, make your commitment unconditional so that no deals or compromises can be negotiated at a later point.

By making this deal with yourself, you will have eliminated all potential "feedback" that will try to talk you out of your contract. Once the terms are set in stone, there will be no room to deviate from them.

Because you are following truth, there will be a constant inspiration to endure throughout the week, despite the constant temptations of your thoughts to compromise or quit. Because your feelings tell you that you are doing the right thing, you will be more resistant to taking the easy way out.

As the week progresses, you will notice a growing sense of accomplishment. You will begin to feel that you are no longer at the mercy of your thoughts. Discipline is like any other habit—the more you do it, the easier it becomes.

EXERCISE 2: Not doing what you should be doing

Now think of something that is *not* a part of your daily habits that you feel (truth) you should be doing on a daily basis. Perhaps you would like to keep your room cleaner, get up earlier in the morning, or spend more time with family or friends.

Whatever is lacking, you are the one who knows. Again, take a few minutes to think about those things you would like to incorporate into your daily life. If it's running two miles every morning, then make a contract with yourself for just the next week that "rain or shine, I will get up in the morning and run my two miles."

Again, if this commitment is made with the understanding that there will be no compromises or deals, then there will be no temptation to take the easy way out as each day progresses.

These exercises will prove a number of valuable things to you. First, you will notice that your motivation to fulfill these exercises will increase because you are working in *conjunction* with truth. Secondly, due to the black and white nature of your decision to follow through with these challenges "at all costs," there will no longer be any desire to compromise or negotiate an easy way out. Lastly, with each passing day, the discomfort of breaking old habits and creating new habits will be replaced by feelings of pride and achievement.

FASTING: THE ONE DAY TEST

If making a one week commitment seems overwhelming to you, then the act of fasting will teach you the same lessons and offer you the same insight in a twenty-four hour period. Fasting is an ancient custom that serves many purposes.

Fasting allows the body to purify. Because the majority of our diet is filled with chemicals and saturated fats, fasting gives the body an extra day to rest from the constant work of removing toxins.

Fasting instills in us a sense of appreciation for those things that are taken for granted. Once we see the value of a single piece of fruit, we will begin to see the value in other things in our life.

Fasting will teach you that you can do anything you want if you commit your mind to it. Perhaps this is the most important lesson of fasting. Because fasting is so difficult, it will be a true test of our self-control and perserverance. It will prove how strong we really are. At the end of the twenty-four hour period, our overwhelming feeling will not be, "Thank goodness, it's over," but, "Thank goodness I chose to do this!"

EXERCISE 3: A day of fasting

Select a day to fast that is advantageous to your schedule. It may *not* be in your best interest to pick a work day, since we often need lunch or dinner to relax. Instead, pick a day when you are not working, when you are not as formatted by lunch and dinner.

No matter what day you choose though, your fast will always start and finish in the morning. For example, if you choose Saturday morning to begin your fast, then Sunday morning would mark the end of your fast. Thus, all of Saturday would be considered your "fast day," and Sunday morning would be considered your "break fast."

Lastly, realize that once your fast has started, there's no turning back. Go to bed the night before with the mind-set that you are welcoming this exercise as a personal challenge. If you see this as an opportunity to develop your focus, you will spend the majority of the day *observing* the temptations of your thoughts rather than fighting them. This is a side benefit of this exercise.

Note: If you're on medication or feel that an abrupt change in your diet may be detrimental to your health, please consult your physician or nutritionist before attempting a fast. Also, I highly recommend that you supplement your fast by drinking as much water as possible. This will give the body some nourishment and prevent you from feeling completely drained and dehydrated.

A Final Word on Discipline

The first step in taking control of our mind rather than it controlling us is through the application of discipline. Discipline will help us reduce unnecessary *active* thinking and enable us to make decisions based not on comfort, but on truth.

By challenging our lazy tendencies, discipline will allow us to welcome problems rather than resist them. Thus, all situations can be used to our advantage, rather than to our disadvantage. The more difficult a problem is, the greater will be our reward in conquering it.

CHAPTER 6

Mental Training

Because mental training is an art form, it should never be limited by a set of rules. What's good for one person may not necessarily be good for another. Therefore, the following process is the converging of several techniques, designed to reap the benefits of many practices.

"Tapping In"

The question isn't *whether* or not you have talents and abilities. The question is *how* much do you have and how much are you *failing* to apply?

As you'll recall, your athletic talents and creative abilities reside in your Unconscious, the home of all of your natural and creative resources, and are processed by the right hemisphere of the brain. These resources are unlimited. But for athletes they often seem illusive, hidden, or out of grasp at the times we need them most.

In Chapter 1 we identified the stumbling blocks to getting in touch with our natural resources as overthinking, congestion and distractions. In Chapter 4 we learned how to inactively clear the mind through meditation; in Chapter 5 we learned how to actively clear the mind though discipline.

In this chapter we will learn how to tap into our natural resources on a consistent basis.

This will be done in two stages: first by *inactively* clearing the path to our natural resources, much as a sculptor reveals his image by *removing* pieces of stone; and second, by *actively* "re-circuiting" or "re-shaping" the muscle memory in our brain, much as an artist paints a picture on a blank canvass.

This double-faceted approach of clearing and then enhancing the mind is the Mental Training process.

MENTAL TRAINING AND MEDITATION

The Mental Training process incorporates many of the same principles as Meditation. Both require that we set aside twenty minutes each day, that we train in the same place at the same time, that we wear comfortable clothing, and that we emphasize the role of the breath.

But where meditation is based on inaction, mental training utilizes both inaction and action. Where meditation has typically one objective: to follow one's breath, or to simply "be," mental training has two objectives: to clear the mind and ultimately, through various exercises, enhance it.

Mental training, like meditation, is a "practice." And like meditation one can never say, "I've mastered it and therefore don't need to do it anymore." It's like a weight lifter's physique. If one doesn't work at it, one will lose it.

Therefore, you should plan to supplement meditation with mental training on a daily basis. If time is an issue and you can only allocate twenty minutes a day, then spend one day on meditation and the next on mental training. *But be sure that you are spending at least twenty minutes a day on one or the other.*

THE KEYS TO MENTAL TRAINING

Foundation

Mental training is a *cumulative* process. This means you must be proficient at each step before moving on to the next. Therefore, don't be so goal-oriented that you rush through the steps. You must have mastered each step before moving on to the next. As with any endeavor, your level of success is directly proportional to the strength of your Foundation.

Commitment

Most endeavors are abandoned in the early stages because people are looking for immediate gratification, and if they don't get it, they quit. If you are to gain full advantage from the mental training process, you must look past the short term gain to the long term results. The journey up a steep mountain may seem long and uneventful, but once on top, you will see the beauty of the entire valley below.

MAKING THE TRANSITION: "A" STATE AND "B" STATE

"A" state and "B" state are arbitrary terms used to define our public time and our private time.

"A" state is our public time.

This is the time we engage in the normal activity of our lives: eating, sleeping, working, playing, wondering and worrying. "A" state is not good or bad; it's both good and bad. It's everything we know and everything we do; it's almost all of our waking hours.

"A" state is our *conscious* time. It is our time to analyze, hypothesize, and theorize, to be simple or complex, to pass judgement or voice our opinions. "A" state is that part of our day when we are conscious of all acts and all activities.

"B" state is our private time.

It is that time of our day set aside to let go of all internal worries, doubts and fears, to suspend all external concerns, demands and responsibilities. It is our time to work on ourselves, to bring our focus inward. It is our time for quieting and calming the winds of thought in order to let ourselves simply "be."

"B" state is our *Unconscious* time. It is a place to cultivate and nourish the core of our existence; a space where we can delve into the depths of our mind to gain a deeper understanding of issues that need to be addressed and goals that need to be conquered.

"B" state is our time away from people, the world, obligations. It is a chance to get back to our "original" home base, to wipe the slate clean. By spending time answering only to ourselves, we can begin to know and understand ourselves intimately, away from the influences of society.

Setting aside part of our day for private time will enhance anyone's life, but for an athlete, who must deal with an extraordinary amount of distractions, it is not an option, but a necessity. If we fail to allocate some "private time," then there will be no escape from the constant demands of "A" state. There will be nowhere to run and nowhere to hide from our conscious thoughts. This is why we must stipulate time in our day and reserve space for ourselves.

Allocating time for mental training may seem difficult at first, but once you reap the benefits of a more relaxed, consistent and focused performance, your mental training time or "private time" will be a priority rather than an option. A choice rather than a demand. An opportunity rather than an obligation.

THE PROCESS

The Mental Training process consists of seven stages. The first four stages are intended to put the mind and body into a deep state of relaxation. This is the inactive or *Relaxation* phase. The last three stages are intended to enhance the mind. They constitute the active or *Enhancement* phase. Each of the seven stages has its own exercise, but remember, you must complete each exercise for the suggested number of sessions before proceeding on to the next exercise.

The seven stages are:

Relaxation Phase:
1. Frame of Mind
2. Exaggerated Deep Breaths[1]
3. Exaggerated Deep Breaths/Auto Suggestion
4. Imagery—Non-sports environment

Enhancement Phase:
5. Imagery—Sports environment
6. Visualization/Lanes
7. Narrowing the Focus

Although the mental training technique is presented in a variety of stages or "movements," once practiced it will flow like a good book or movie. In a sense, because it is not confined to one monotonous or tedious exercise, you will find it easy to maintain a level of "freshness" and enjoyment.

---

1   Exaggerated Deep Breaths will also be used at the end of each training session to culminate the process.

STAGE I: FRAME OF MIND

When was the last time you played in a game or match without stretching or warming up? In other words, when was the last time you just showed up at game time, cold turkey, without any prior preparation? If you are like most athletes, it would be inconceivable for you to skip your pre-game preparation. Not only wouldn't you be physically and mentally prepared, but you would greatly increase the likelihood of getting injured. All athletes know the importance of pre-game preparation, of fine-tuning their skills before they take the field. In fact, there is usually as much emphasis put on pre-game preparation as there is on the game itself. Mental training must be approached in the same manner. Your sessions, like your performance, will be a direct reflection of your *preparation*.

Therefore, we don't want to "jump" into our mental training sessions without taking a few minutes to first prepare and alert the mind. It would be unrealistic to close our eyes and expect to displace a turbulent mind with a calm mind at a moment's notice.

We need to spend a few minutes to make the break from "A" state to "B" state. We need to close the door on the past and future and open the door to the present. We need to bring all of our attention, all of our focus to the *here* and *now*.

Frame of Mind, or our pre-session preparation, allows us to make a smooth transition from the distractions of "A" state to the privacy of "B" state. It's a deal that allows us to suspend thought for a predetermined length of time. If we fail to make this smooth transition, chances are that we will bring a "busy" mind into our mental training session and dilute its effectiveness.

Getting into the proper Frame of Mind is a precursor to the entire mental training session. It is symbolic of stretching before we run, of warming-up before we throw.

EXERCISE 1—Frame of Mind

Recommended Sessions: 4 (twice each day for two days)
Duration in Minutes: 5

As with meditation, wear comfortable clothes, select a quiet place, sit in a comfortable position, and take a minute or two to alert your mind that you are about to enter "B" state.

Remember, this is your private time, so tell yourself, "Whatever has gone on prior to this twenty minutes, and whatever will go on after these twenty minutes does not concern me; I have the remainder of the day to deal with these issues. All that matters to me now is the present moment, since this is the only time that I am in complete control." Put all thoughts, both good and bad, on the shelf and channel all of your energy into the present moment. Remind yourself that this is an opportunity to nourish your mind and body.

Once you feel that you have genuinely brought all of your attention and focus to the here and now, you will have made a "clean break" from "A" state to "B" state.

Now start becoming aware of your breathing. Follow its pace or simply observe it for as long as you can without your attention becoming distracted. If your mind does become distracted, then simply bring your focus back to your breathing (it helps to think of your breath as your partner). Make it a goal to increase your awareness with each passing breath. Use your breath as a guide and continue to follow it for at least five minutes.

By entering the right frame of mind at the beginning of each session, you will alert your mind that you are about to enter your "private time," or your focusing time, and that you are not to be disturbed. This will allow you to begin the training process with an undivided mind—a physical and mental awareness that the following twenty minutes have been "reserved" for intense, concentrated effort.

Comment: In order to attain maximum results from our the mental training process, we must first make the separation from "A" state to "B" state. If your mind is not prepped, then the remainder of the technique will be of diminished value.

STAGE II: EXAGGERATED DEEP BREATHS

In the case of the archer, his success isn't based so much on his aim, his ability to hit a specific target, or even to outdo his opponent. In the art of archery, the archer succeeds or fails in relation to his ability to keep his breathing in harmony with his mind and body.

—EUGEN HERRIGEL

As the breath goes, so goes the athlete. If the athlete is to master his sport, he must first attune himself to his breathing.

Just as diaphramatic breathing was the basis of Meditation, it is a fundamental part of Mental Training. But in the mental training process, we utilize a distinct form of diaphragmatic breathing known as *exaggerated deep breaths*. Exaggerated deep breaths will not only help us relax, but they will be used to signal the start and finish of each mental training session.

The role of breathing cannot be overemphasized in the mental training process, for breathing is perhaps the most essential and fundamental process of all human beings. Like a silent partner, it is with you every step of the way. If this partner is calm and under control, then likewise you will be calm and under control. If it is tense and stressed, then you will be tense and stressed. Your breathing is a constant measure from moment to moment of your state of being, of your state of mind.

Following one's breath may seem trivial in comparison with the other physical and mental preparations of an athlete, but the fact is your breathing has a *direct* effect on your performance. When it comes down to match point, or bases loaded with two outs in the bottom of the ninth, the athlete who is likely to prevail is the one whose breathing is calm and under control, a sure sign that *he* is calm and under control.

Unfortunately, in the West, where physical preparation has been the *only* preparation, the role of one's breath has been lost in the shuffle. In fact, most Western athletes are completely unaware of the role breathing plays in their performance.

In the East, where one's performance symbolizes one's approach to life, the control and pace of one's breath is of central importance. It serves as one's balance point throughout the entire performance; a constant reminder that if "it" is out of control then the performer is likely to follow suit.

EXERCISE 2—Exaggerated Deep Breaths

Recommended Sessions: 6 (twice each day for three days)
Duration in Minutes: 10

Begin this exercise as you will begin every exercise, by taking a few moments to make the break from "A" state to "B" state (Frame of Mind).

Now observe the manner or pace of your breathing. Concentrate on your diaphragm or stomach region and notice where the origin of your breath begins and where it ends. Chances are that a movement in your chest or shoulders will supersede that of your diaphragm. For now, this is of no concern. What really matters is that you are allowing your breath to operate without conscious intervention, somewhat as your eyes will blink on their own. In a sense, your breath should actually be "breathing" you.

After watching your breath for a few minutes, start focusing more intently on your diaphragm or stomach area. Begin to pull air in through your nose, *allowing* your stomach area to soften and expand outward at its own pace. Try to imagine that your stomach is inflating like a balloon.

You may have a tendency to roll your shoulders forward or lift your chest, so try to imagine that your shoulders are either cemented to the back of your chair, or the surface of whatever you happen to be sitting/lying on.

If you are sitting in a position without any support, then imagine that your shoulders are cemented in place. This will take your chest and shoulders out of play and allow your diaphragm to do all of the work.

Once your diaphragm completely fills with air, your chest cavity can begin to get involved with the inhalation process. But the chest cavity should not be involved until after the diaphragm has been adequately filled.

The inhalation phase of the breath should be taken in very deliberately and with minimum effort. As the diaphragm completely fills, hold on to the air for a long pause (just long enough to create a tiny bit of tension). Again, you want to be sure that you are exhaling or releasing the breath through your nose deliberately, proportionately, and calmly.

Though it takes a lot of patience, the air must be exhaled at a very slow rate and there should be as much air dispensing at the beginning of the exhalation phase as there is at the end. After the air has been completely exhausted, pause for a moment and immediately begin to inhale another breath. (Note: If you have some problem inhaling or exhaling out of your nasal passage, then follow the same format, only inhaling and exhaling out of your mouth).

This style of breathing is called *exaggerated* breathing. The cycle of a full inhalation and exhalation is called an *exaggerated deep breath*. Although the format parallels the most correct way to breathe, it is done so in an exaggerated manner. By breathing in an exaggerated manner, the body begins to "measure" the breath and become impressioned by it. Because this method of breathing is also physiologically healthier, the body quickly adjusts Unconsciously.

For mental training purposes, five exaggerated deep breaths will be taken at the beginning to mark your entrance point and five at the end will mark your exit point. Exaggerated deep breaths on the "way in" will get you off on the right foot by helping you to quickly relax, and exaggerated deep breaths on the "way out" will help you finish strong.

Because you will always start and finish your sessions with exaggerated deep breaths, you will have formed a set of "bookends." The remainder of your training period will represent the "story."

Comment: Diaphragmatic or belly breathing is a way of life to the artists of the Far East. It is a constant force during competition, and a constant reminder away from the arena. Once mastered, your breathing will serve as a foundation, a home base, and a balance point regardless of where you happen to be.

STAGE III: EXAGGERATED DEEP BREATHS/AUTO-SUGGESTION: ENTRY AND EXIT WORDS

Since *exaggerated deep breaths* will serve as the start and finish of each of the following exercises, it will be beneficial for our minds to fasten on to a word that will signal both the beginning and end of the session.

By suggesting a word to yourself such as "calm" or "release" on each exhalation at the beginning of each session, your mind will ready itself for the mental training process that is about to begin. Likewise, by using a word like "focused" or "prepared" on each exhalation at the end of each session, the mind will ready itself to return to "A" state.

Other words that you might choose for the beginning or "entrance" stage of the session include: Peace, Calm, Free, Release, Clear, Focus. Words for the end or "exit" stage of the session might be: Focused, Prepared, Energized, Relaxed, Natural.

These words will act as a stimulus for a conditioned response. The mind will "register" the image or feeling that is associated with these words, and that will trigger the mind-set we plan to attain. The ability of a word to trigger a specific response is called *auto-suggestion*.

Auto-suggestion serves many important roles in the mental training process. In conjunction with your deep breathing, it leads you into a deeper form of relaxation. And, as we will discuss later in the chapter, it will be used to trigger your focus *away* from your training sessions.

EXERCISE 3—Exaggerated Deep Breaths/Auto Suggestion

Recommended Sessions: 6 (twice each day for three days)
Duration in Minutes: 10

Begin, as always, by putting yourself in the proper Frame of Mind. Make sure that you have put your "A" state on the shelf and that your entire focus is in the present moment. (Remember, as your Frame of Mind goes, so goes the success of your mental training).

Next, take five exaggerated deep breaths, emphasizing the "entrance" word you have chosen (calm, peace, etc.) to yourself on the exhale. Remember, the word should last for the entire duration of the exhale.

After you have taken five exaggerated deep breaths in this manner, allow your breathing to return to its normal pace and rhythm and simply *observe* it *without* any effort to control it. As you'll see, your breath will find its own rhythm, its own happy medium.

After spending five minutes or so becoming acquainted with the natural pace of your breath, you will now want to "cue" the mind and body that your mental training session is coming to a close. This will be done with five more exaggerated deep breaths, this time choosing an "exit" word (focused, prepared) that is conducive to culminating your session or finishing strong.

Comment: Although some consider auto-suggestion a "mystical" phenomenon, it is precisely the manner in which hypnosis works. It is the power of suggestion that aligns itself with your Unconscious, so that even if you're not aware of specific suggestions, your Unconscious is always aware. Words are important. By saying "I will do something" as opposed to "I hope I can do something," you have already set the tone for getting it done.

STAGE IV: IMAGERY—NON-SPORTS ENVIRONMENT

Imagery is the fourth stage in the mental training process. It will allow us to enter a state of complete relaxation by utilizing our imagination to create pleasant images in our mind, rather than unpleasant thoughts.

By imaging specific "scenes" with a relaxed mind, and putting ourselves in a comfortable environment, we will learn how to trust the mind and body to simply *be*, without conscious intervention.

The following scenes are designed to sharpen your creative skills and allow your imagination to run free. In order to get the most out of these exercises, try to be as detailed as possible. Use your senses to hear sounds, see colors or smell aromas; your emotions to feel joy, excitement, or the serenity of being at peace with yourself.

The River

Picture yourself resting against a rock alone on a mountain top, free from the troubles, obligations and worries of everyday life. Recognize that there is nothing around you except the sounds and sights of nature: the trickle of a stream, the whisper of a soft gentle breeze, the serene glow of a white moon. Imagine the crackling of a campfire, the heat creeping into your bones.

This is your private land, your secret space that no one else knows about.

To the side of the mountain is a tame and friendly river. It traverses down the side of the mountain at a calm and steady pace. At the bottom of the mountain, the mouth of the river merges into a still and quiet lake.

Now board your raft at the top of the mountain and let the river carry you down the mountainside. As you make your way down, if there are any remnants of thoughts or worries, put them in a box and toss them over the side of your raft. As you continue on your way down the mountain, continue to trust the flow of the river. Don't be concerned with where you are going. Let go of your controls and let the river make all of the turns for you. As you begin to approach the mouth of the lake, notice how motionless the lake is. Its surface, like glass, is so smooth that it casts a perfect image of yourself. Now begin to associate your mind with the characteristics of the lake. Let it be still, quiet, motionless.

The Falling Leaf

Put yourself in an environment to your liking. Perhaps you are in the woods on a crystal clear day with a powder blue sky overhead and a gentle breeze to soothe your face. Now imagine that you are a leaf high atop a tree, gliding and floating as you make your way down to the ground.

Because you are as light as a feather, the ride is gentle, the turns are graceful. Begin putting more and more faith into the currents of the wind as you make your way down ever so slowly, ever so gently. As you float to the ground, allow the feelings of "letting go" continue to immerse you. Don't be concerned with where you are or what you are doing, but simply take in the feeling of freedom and the trust of letting go.

The Pebble

When a pebble has been thrown into a lake, it falls aimlessly and effortlessly through the still, calm water. Detached from everything, the pebble slowly descends to the bottom of the lake where it settles quietly on a bed of fine sand. Now imagine you are a pebble, aimlessly drifting through the quiet stillness of a blue lake. Allow yourself to descend through the gentle water until you come to a comfortable landing on the lake floor. No longer pushed or pulled by thoughts, allow your mind to come to perfect rest, just as your body has come to perfect rest.

EXERCISE 4—Imagery: Non-Sports Environment

Recommended Sessions: 4 (once each day for four days)
Duration in Minutes : 15

Begin as always by getting into your "B" state frame of mind. Now, in conjunction with the exhalation phase of your breath, verbalize your auto-suggestion entry word to yourself and try to conjure those feelings that you associate with that word. Next, choose one of the previous predetermined scenes and "let go" in your non-sports environment.

When you have spent fifteen minutes in peaceful relaxation, use your five exaggerated deep breaths with your exit word to end the session.

Comment: Being able to use our imagination is a skill like any other. Because our imagination can take us anywhere we like, creative imagery can be used for a variety of purposes. For the sake of "letting go" and relaxation, we have used images that the general population can relate to...nature. In this next section we will use creative imagery for a more specific reason—to put us into the comforts of our sports environment.

STAGE V: IMAGERY: SPORTS ENVIRONMENT

Now that you've had some practice at "letting go" in a relaxed and peaceful environment, it is time to transfer these same feelings of comfort and relaxation into our home away from home...our sports environment. This is the transition stage of the mental training process. In this exercise we will be moving from the deep *inactive* relaxation of letting go, to the *active* enhancement of the mind. By using creative imagery we will not only put ourselves us into an athlete's forum, but into an athlete's mind.

Because the serious athlete spends at least one third of his or her life on the playing field, nothing could be of greater value than to find peace of mind in this environment. Once we put ourselves on the playing field, we can put ourselves in any specific situation that needs work. We can put ourself in the batter's box or on the putting green. We can practice hitting a curve ball or sinking a three foot putt.

But being comfortable in our sports environment is only half the goal of this exercise. It is also important to image *your attitude* in this environment. Before you can do this, you must ask yourself, "What attitude do I display when I am *excelling* at my game? Am I intense, relaxed, graceful, confident or determined? What compels me to compete and to win? What qualities do I portray when I am performing *at my best*? This is what I call your "game face." Be honest about your feelings, but focus only on those feelings that are *positive*.

Where "letting go" was the goal of Exercise #4, entering our sports environment and creating a game face attitude is the goal of Exercise 5.

Just as an astronaut learns to feel comfortable in outer space by simulating a weightless environment, the athlete will learn to feel comfortable on the playing field through imagery. Remember, the more realistic your feelings are, the more effective your imaging will be.

EXERCISE 5—Imagery: Sports Environment

Recommended Sessions: 4 (once each day for four days)
Duration in Minutes: 15

Begin by getting into your "B" state frame of mind. Take five exaggerated deep breaths, repeating your entry word on the long exhale. Imagine your scene: flowing with the river, floating like a leaf, or falling like a pebble. Now you are ready to move smoothly and comfortably to your sports environment. Because your mind and body are coming from a place of serenity and tranquility, your sports environment will take on similar characteristics. See yourself on the field, on the court, on the course.

Since the brain is actually programming or "circuiting" the images that you are creating, it is of supreme importance to be as detailed as possible. Ask yourself, "What characteristics of my sports environment make me feel comfortable and at ease?" Fill in your surroundings by appealing to as many senses and emotions as possible. See the grass under your feet. Is it slightly damp, dry, or plush? Feel the warmth of the sun on your skin. Is there a breeze or a light chill in the air? Is the playing surface well manicured?

Like a painter and his canvas, create your environment in vivid colors, exact details. Feel the "gratification" or "joy" of being in an environment that allows you to display your art. You are the producer, director and actor in this "scene," so make it as appealing as possible.

Once you are comfortable in your sports environment, it is time to put on your "game face." Since attitude means everything to a performer, be sure to take the necessary time to see yourself displaying all of the *positive* components of your attitude (confidence, grace, determination). See yourself realistically, experience each positive attribute.

When you feel that you have created the right setting and the right attitude, take five exaggerated deep breaths, using your exit word on the exhale, and return to "A" state.

Comment: Putting yourself in your sports environment and imaging your game-face attitude will not only make you feel comfortable with your surroundings and yourself, but it will create the attitude and mind-set that is ideal for next stage in the Mental Training Process: Visualization.

STAGE VI: VISUALIZATION:
THE ENHANCEMENT OF THE MIND

In Stages 1 through 4 of the Mental Training process, we learned to calm, quiet and relax the mind. We freed-up all the tension associated with daily stress. We erased all of the writing (congestion) on the blackboard.

In Stage 5 we began the active phase of our mental training. Through creative imagery, we became comfortable in our sports environment with our game face attitude.

Here in Stage 6, we will take a further step into the realm of active enhancement. Through Visualization, we will learn to impression our minds with those images (visuals) that will sharpen our mental skills.

Visualization is the pay-off of all of the previous exercises. It is the icing on the cake. If done properly, it will help your physical game as much as *physical* practice. But like physical practice, it requires time, dedication and perseverance.

What is Visualization and Why does it work?

Visualization, in theory, is nothing more than *mental* muscle memory. Because the mind transforms specific images and sounds into stored frequencies, your nervous system will "act" on specific impulses as if you had physically practiced that skill. In theory, the more you visualize a specific image, sound or color, the deeper it becomes imprinted in your nervous system, and the more likely you are to duplicate it as a conditioned reflex.

The brain, like a computer, is sensitive to the "messages" associated with these frequencies, and when faced with real life situations, the brain will naturally reconstruct a particular stored memory somewhat as a computer will "respond" to a particular program. Fortunately, we, as human beings, are not stuck for life with one program. If we wish, we can modify our present program, or create a new program.

Like a computer and its electronic messages, the human brain communicates through neurotransmitters. If the computer has a short circuit, a bug in the system, or simply malfunctions, it must be "rewired" to correct this flaw. Likewise, if the brain has a malfunction, a breakdown or an abundance of mental congestion, then similarly, the system must be cleared and put back in sync.

Now that we have cleared our system, it is time to "inscribe" our program. Through Visualization, we will "recircuit" the mind; we will imprint those specific images that will benefit our attitude, approach, and focus as both athletes and as human beings.

Locking in: Visualizing Our Lanes and Narrowing Our Focus

Now that we have an insight into the dynamics of Visualization, what is it that we are actually Visualizing?

Visualization can be used in many ways, but we shall concentrate on only two: the development of accuracy and precision through *Lanes*; and the elimination of external distractions by *Narrowing the Focus*. Getting a feel for these two tactics will enable you to fortify your internal skills while eliminating external distractions.

Lanes

No matter what sport you've played, you've experienced the phenomenon of *lanes.*

In baseball, pitchers always "imagine" the flight of the ball from their release point to the catcher's mitt. This path is, in essence, a "lane." A basketball player sees his jump shot traveling from his fingertips through the bottom of the net; a golfer must account for certain "breaks" or bends in the green when putting; a place kicker will imagine the flight of the ball through the uprights. All athletes visualize "lanes" whether they are aware of it or not.

Visualizing Lanes is advantageous because lanes are very precise. By placing your attention on a specific point (lane), the mind (circuits) can begin to look past the "big picture" (general) and focus sharply on the details (specific). For example, if a pitcher wants to become more consistent with a pitch to the outside corner, he could begin to Visualize the flight of the ball from point A (release point) to point B, the catcher's glove at the outside corner of the plate.

This "formatted" path or lane becomes "circuited" in the brain. In time, as you begin to repeat this vision of seeing the flight of the ball consistently in its lane, you will begin to *feel* the success of "driving" this lane at will. The more you "see" the success of your lanes, the more likely the brain is going to elicit this response and *follow through* with this predetermined outcome.

Visualizing your lanes is designed for a precise result. At this point in your mental training, the mind will be very receptive to the following exercises because you have cleared the congestion and prepared it to relearn specific "messages."

EXERCISE 6—Visualization/Lanes

Recommended Sessions: 4 (one each day for four days)
Duration in Minutes : 20

Begin by getting into your "B" state. Take your exaggerated deep breaths, repeating your entry word on the exhale. Imagine your relaxation scene, move into your sports environment, and put on your game-face. Now you are ready to "work" on that part of your game that needs attention or lacks consistency.

Once you are comfortable in your sports environment, define with your mind where your desired lane starts and where it ends. Now try to imagine yourself "driving" along this path. Naturally, it will take some concentration and effort, but you'll begin to notice that your lane will actually *help* you keep your attention on it. Remember, you will not see any obstacles if you keep your eyes on your lane.

As you begin to get a "feel" for your lane, be as detailed as possible. Again, use your senses and emotions to help validate the reality of the messages to your brain. Creativity counts as much as the actual development of the lane. See the baseball snow white with bright red laces. See the hockey puck jet black, ice cold and hard as stone.

When your time is up, take your exaggerated deep breaths, repeating your exit word on the exhale, and return to "A" state.

Comment: Visualization is a very delicate and sensitive exercise. It takes more finesse than it does grind. So *quality* is always more important than quantity. Don't get caught up with a feeling that you need to see your lane a hundred times. This only creates unnecessary tension and effort. It is better to see your lane five or ten times if it is visualized with creativity, composure and precision.

Lanes are particularly helpful in the following activities:

- Baseball—Hitting, Pitching, Throwing (outfielders and infielders)
- Tennis—Serving, Volleying, Ground strokes, Net play
- Golf—Putting, Chipping, Driving
- Football—Passing, Receiving, Kicking
- Hockey—Wrist shots, Slap shots, Goaltending
- Basketball—Shooting

STAGE VII: NARROWING THE FOCUS

"Blackening In"

If you've ever looked through a kaleidoscope, a telescope, or even a pair of binoculars, you've probably noticed that the images you are viewing seem to have uncanny definition. In the case of binoculars, the magnifying lens helps make the images appear clearer and sharper. But less obvious and even more important is the role the *absence* of light plays on the appearance of the image. This "blackening effect," or the voiding of peripheral stimulation, allows the viewed image to appear richer, sharper and more in focus to the optic nerve (that part of the eye that sends messages to the brain).

But unlike the "controlled setting" of binoculars, there are many "stimuli" that exist in the "uncontrolled setting" of an athlete's environment. Peripheral distractions come with the territory of performing in a public arena. Fans, media, scouts, recruiters, even family and friends can and will ultimately divert our focus.

Where the development of "lanes" is used to improve specific physical skills, *Narrowing the Focus* or "Blackening-in" will serve to eliminate external distractions that exist *outside* of your lanes. Blackening-in will create a "pitch black," stimulus-free background that will both heighten the clarity of the desired image and remove the background details that normally vie for your attention during performance.

By having these potential distractions removed from your peripheral vision, you will be able to focus on the task at hand. In the case of a baseball pitcher, he will be able to confine his line of focus from the "general" (the stadium) to the "specific" (60 feet 6 inches). All background details will cease to exist and his sole focus will be on his lane.

Because the background is "void" of all factors, lanes will not only be sharper or brighter, but they will be more easily grasped. Instead of trying to visualize your lanes on a television screen that is already filled with data, Blackening-in will allow you to turn the television set off.

Once you learn to Blacken-in, everything outside of your lane will be eliminated. Thus, you will only be aware of the batter's box on a baseball diamond, the ice of a hockey rink, the fairway of the golf course, the wood of the basketball court. Everything else will be out of sight...out of mind, and you will be able to stay within yourself.

EXERCISE 7—Narrowing the Focus

Recommended Sessions: 6 (one each day for six days)
Duration in Minutes: 20

Put yourself in your correct frame of mind, take your exaggerated deep breaths with your entry word, and move directly into the comforts of your sports environment. Take a minute or two to identify every potential distraction that may have disturbed you in the past (scouts, fans, media, friends, family). Now put them in the stands, knowing this is the last time you ever need to address them. Once you've allowed them to find their seats, turn off the house lights in the stands, or simply take a paintbrush and Blacken-in everything and anything that exists outside of your line of focus.

As the distractions on the periphery of your lanes cease to exist, the lanes themselves will take on a more vivid image. This "brightness" of your lane will provide a clearer and more concise "circuitry" to the brain.

Note: In this exercise, Blackening-in should be done *before* visualizing your lanes. You will only need to go through the process of identifying and blackening-in your distractions a couple of times. Once they have disappeared it will no longer be necessary to do this exercise unless distractions again creep up around your lanes.

When you have completed visualizing your lanes, take your exaggerated deep breaths accompanied by your exit word and return to "A" state.

Comment: Narrowing the Focus (Blackening-in) is a process that can be applied to a wide and unlimited range of areas of your game. We have presented two of the most beneficial: to sharpen and brighten your lanes, and to eliminate all peripheral distractions. Once you have learned to Blacken-in your lanes, it will no longer matter *where* you are performing or for whom you are performing. Your art has been reduced to mastering your lanes.

RETRIEVING OUR PROGRAM: UNCONSCIOUS TRIGGERS

Before we conclude the Mental Training Process we must consider one more factor that aids this process: *Unconscious Triggers.*

Imagine you are listening to one of your all-time favorite albums. It is an album that you know inside and out, note for note, word for word. You know it so well that when you hear the end of one song, you automatically hear the beginning of the next. In other words, you've heard the "transition" so many times that *Unconsciously*, the winding down of one song *triggers* the beginning of the next song before it actually begins to play.

The same can be said of the mind's ability to "feed-back" off of other Unconscious triggers. As you practice your mental training techniques, your mind will develop its own "songs." Because your "B" state is essentially a recording of your own "album" with your own set of songs (deep breaths, images, visuals, etc.), you can use exaggerated deep breaths *away* from your training sessions as an Unconscious trigger.

Again, if we look at the evolution of the mental training process, exaggerated deep breaths serve as the "book ends" of our "B" state. Thus, imagery and visualization techniques serve as our "story." Since our story is preceded and completed by exaggerated *deep breaths*, it would follow that exaggerated deep breaths *away* from our sessions will elicit a learned or conditioned response. Therefore, exaggerated deep breaths will serve as a trigger that Unconsciously prompts our story much in the same manner that the ending of one song of an album brings into our mind the beginning of the next song.

Whether you are conscious of it or not, exaggerated deep breaths will not only physiologically relax your mind and muscles, but they will "call up" all of the characteristics that are manifested during the mental training process ("B" state): a clear mind, a disciplined mind, a determined attitude, and the accuracy and precision of your lanes.

A Final Word

The beauty of Mental Training is that you can work on your game without ever leaving the comfortable confines of your own home. It is unique in that one's success is not based on raw physical talent, but on dedication, commitment and perseverance. All it requires is twenty minutes per day. Every day.

CHAPTER 7

Game Management: Philosophy on the Field

Winning is a by-product of learning how to play with the game, not at it.

PEAK EXPERIENCES: ARE THEY REALLY THAT UNIQUE?

All athletes have experienced it at one time or another. A feeling that occurs when everything begins to fall into place. There is a quiet aura around us, a state of "effortless" control as the mind goes on automatic pilot. All conscious activity temporarily ceases to exist. Batters say that the baseball looks the size of a beach ball. Pitchers say that the catcher appears closer, the plate wider. A golfer visualizes his chip landing close to the pin. A basketball player feels the bottom of the net with the tips of his fingers.

The athlete *expects* perfect results, and for a short time, he or she will get them.

Athletes describe this feeling by saying, "I'm in a groove," "I'm on a roll," or "I'm Unconscious." They are having a peak experience, an optimal state of mind where their natural instincts and reactions have taken over and they find themselves *flowing* with the game instead of playing *at* it.

But why do these peak experiences happen so infrequently? Are they "special" states of mind that are only available to us by chance?

As we will see, they do not have to be.

When we look at the make-up of peak experiences we will notice something ironic: the state of mind that accompanies these experiences is actually quite *common*; it is a state of mind that we can all relate to on a daily basis.

All of us have become lost in a suspenseful movie, or absorbed by a good book. If we're doing something we like, the time seems to fly by. At the end of an enjoyable party, someone will ask "where has the time gone?" And we all know how music can remove us from time and space. If the basic make-up of a peak experience is a feeling that "all conscious activity ceases to exist as the mind goes on automatic pilot," then such experiences are not "special" but *natural*. The truth of the matter is that we do not have to attain a "higher" state of mind to achieve a peak experience. We only have to enter a state of mind where we are *reacting* spontaneously, where we are performing without conscious intervention, where we are playing *Unconsciously*.

I call this state of mind "being in the flow."

Although athletes believe that this feeling of "being in the flow" can only be attained on "game days," the truth is that athletes will more often experience this feeling during practice. For it is here the athlete feels most relaxed.

Because practice is "nothing special," and there are no real consequences at stake, the athlete doesn't feel the need to "try harder." Because the athlete has less pressure and tension to contend with, the natural movements of his body will begin to take over, until he finds himself playing Un-consciously.

Although we may not be able to maintain a "peak experience" throughout our entire performance, we can maintain the state of mind that leaves us open to one. We can learn how to stay "in the flow."

GAME DAY: FORCES THAT TAKE US OUT OF THE FLOW

Due to the many pressures and distractions that come with the territory of "game days," there are many forces trying to take us out of the flow. Therefore, we must identify these forces and learn how to deal with them.

DEAD TIME

Perhaps the single biggest reason we are taken off our game is because there are "gaps" in our performance. It is this in-between or "dead time" that breaks our rhythm or flow. Unlike musicians or dancers, who can rely on a continuous rhythm or melody to keep them in sync, an athlete must often wait between shots, swings and throws.

For example, a golfer may have up to three or four minutes of dead time between shots. Batters come to the plate once every thirty minutes; place kickers may go an entire quarter or half without a single field goal attempt; and "free" throws give basketball players just enough "free" time to start thinking.

If we are to stay in the flow then we must begin to use our dead time to our advantage. We can do this in three ways.

First, we can utilize the deep breathing technique set forth in the previous chapter. By taking a few deep breaths and following the pace of our breathing, our body will relax, our mind will slow down, and we will alleviate the onset of distractive thoughts. Second, we can identify random thoughts as constructive or non-constructive. If they are constructive, we can allow them to guide us like the wings of a bird. If they are non-constructive, we must *let them go* from whence they came.

Third, we can make constructive statements to ourselves, even though our ultimate goal is the *absence* of thinking.

Dead time can be very disruptive to an athlete's performance, but by following these three strategies, we can use dead time to sustain our flow, rather than disrupt it.

Thinking

We have already discussed the functions of the two hemispheres of the brain. You'll remember that our left brain houses our thoughts, and our right brain houses our talents and abilities. Since *thinking* is a left brain phenomenon and *reacting* is a right brain phenomenon, you can now see that if you are preoccupied with your thoughts, your natural reactions cannot take over. If you are in a *conscious* mode, then you are not performing Unconsciously.

This doesn't assume that we *never* need to think.

As mentioned previously, there are times we may need to think in order to neutralize distractive thoughts. But our goal is to maintain a no-thought or Unconscious mode. The surest way to do this is by using deep breaths.

Trying Too Hard: Trying vs Unleashing

Growing up, we've all been told to try our best; to give it our all. Unfortunately, this good advice can have an adverse effect. Because there is so much at stake on game days, "trying our best" can translate to *trying too hard*.

"Trying harder" implies that we are making an *extra* effort, a *conscious* effort that does not arise on its own. If the key ingredient to being "in the flow" is performing Un-consciously, then the very nature of *trying* means we are destroying the natural flow of events with *conscious* input or effort.

Our purpose is to *always* play at our best, and if we are doing that, there is no need to "try harder."

SUPERSTITIONS

"Hope and fear cannot alter the seasons."

—CHOGYAM TRUNGPA

As defined by the dictionary, "a superstition is an *irrational* state of mind that results from an unreasonable fear of the unknown."

In sports, a superstition is any action or thought that is carried out to satisfy the irrational belief that something negative can be avoided, or something positive can be gained, by following a pre-set ritual.

Many athletes swear by their superstitions, and in some cases superstitions can have a beneficial short term result. This is because superstitions help "pacify" unwanted or distractive thinking. They enable us to feel secure that "good things" will follow if we obey or stay consistent with the "rules" of our mind games. And because we believe in our rituals, and are feeling optimistic, chances are we will have some positive results.

But what happens when our superstitions let us down? Usually we will add, remove or change our superstition until we "get it right." This is a desperate cycle that only serves to distract our mind from the real task at hand.

Anyone who has been a prisoner to a superstition knows that there is no such thing as "getting it right." Eventually, our luck begins to fade. In reality, all we're doing is creating an elaborate ritual that will disrupt our flow.

Letting go of superstitions may seem difficult at first, but having them is a constant reminder that we are trying to *manipulate* our *actions* when it should be our sole intention to *trust* our *reactions*.

Game Management:
Principles That Keep Us in the Flow

Now that we are aware of some of the forces trying to take us out of the flow, let's examine some of the principles that will help keep us in the flow.

Trusting Our Instincts

The centipede was happy, quite
Until a toad in fun
Said, "Prey which leg goes after which?"
This worked his mind to such a pitch,
He lay distracted in a ditch,
Considering how to run

—Zenrin Saying

In the above example, where walking was once an Un-conscious task for the centipede, the toad's inquiry suddenly gave him something to be conscious about, something to *think* about. And think he did, until finally he was so distracted, so paralyzed by his very own thoughts, that he eventually lay immobilized in a ditch.

If the centipede only knew to trust his instincts.

As human beings, we sometimes forget that the most basic functions of the mind and body "just happen," by themselves. Our heartbeat, our digestion, our blood flow are not "regulated" by our thoughts. We breathe just because we do. We walk without "consideration" of how to walk. And we can run, hit, catch, shoot, drive, tackle and skate without any input from our thoughts.

We are like the centipede who can perform all of its natural skills perfectly, unless we become entangled by our own web of "considering" how to play.

To be at our best as athletes, we must learn to perform without thinking of our mechanics. We must trust that the right movement or play will "happen" by itself, effortlessly and Unconsciously. We must believe that when we are immersed in the flow of the game, our natural reactions will take over.

PRACTICE LIKE YOU PERFORM: PERFORM LIKE YOU PRACTICE

Have you ever noticed how well we perform when there is nothing on the line? A "casual" game of whiffle ball or a friendly game of over-the-line usually brings out the best in all of us. But once the "real thing" (game day) is upon us, we often become a different person. On "game day," our "game face" changes from one of leisure to one of pressure. The relaxation of the practice field is suddenly displaced by the apprehension of the playing field.

We've all heard about "5 o'clock hitters." These are baseball players who excel during batting practice but struggle at game time. We've all heard golfers talk about "leaving it at the range" when they've had a poor round of golf *after* hitting the ball beautifully at the driving range. These are two examples that sum up the frustration all athletes experience if their mentality changes at game time.

Why do we change our mentality at game time?

During practice, we are free and easy. There is nothing at stake and the stands are empty. Since no one is watching and no one cares, we let loose and even the most difficult task is performed with the greatest of ease.

But once the "flag goes up" and game day is upon us, the environment changes drastically. Now winning and losing is "everything." Now everyone is watching and everyone cares. All of the pressure and tension that was absent on the practice field is present on the playing field. We have lost the naturalness of our practice self.

So again I ask, why do we change our mentality on game days? Why is it so difficult to bring the calmness and security of our practice environment into our performance environment?

The reason is because we have developed two different mind sets: one for the practice field, another for the playing field. Unfortunately, the result of this split mentality is an inconsistent approach, which in turn leads to an inconsistent performance.

Although this "split" mentality is typical of today's athletes, it doesn't have to be.

It is possible to take the same attitude, approach and focus into both settings. We can eliminate the distinction between practicing and performing. We can bring our practice frame of mind into the game, and vice-versa. After all, beneath the uniform, we are always the same athlete. Our flesh and bones do not change. A ball is still a ball, a bat is still a bat.

In the chapter on Mastering Yourself, you learned that you are the one *constant*. Therefore, whether you are practicing or performing is irrelevant.

By eliminating the distinction between practicing and performing, each game and each practice will be of equal importance. As the distinction between practice days and game days diminishes, the consistency of your performance will increase.

I often tell athletes, "Practice like you perform. Perform like you practice." After all, only the circumstances are changing. If you view your sport in this way, it won't matter who you are playing or where you are playing. You will remain consistent.

NOTHING SPECIAL—NOTHING CHANGES

It's the bottom of the ninth inning. You're up at bat with the bases loaded and two outs. Your team is down a run. You realize this situation is especially "important," and the tension begins to mount.

Just as batters put more emphasis on a particular at-bat, tennis players put more emphasis on set point, and golfers on birdie putts. But when we make a given shot "important," a certain play "big," a specific event "crucial," we are putting an extra burden on ourselves. It's as if we have to do something out of the ordinary, something "special."

Anytime we place additional importance on an isolated portion of our performance, we are no longer "letting it happen." We have called our intellect (left brain) into play to remind us to try harder. But as we have seen, "trying harder" only hurts us because it takes us out of our flow.

When we feel the pressure of having to "come through," we become more tense and rigid. Our relaxed focus is suddenly displaced by an intense desire to succeed or an intense fear of failing.

By making situations "special," we are saying that our normal reactions are not good enough. "Letting it happen" turns into "making it happen." We lose trust in our natural ability and look to our conscious effort to help us out.

Once we come to terms with the fact that all situations are of equal importance, that every single play in our performance is a thread in the fabric, then no matter how the situation changes, we will not change.

When we refrain from making situations special, then all circumstances take on equal meaning. Hence, there is no reason to do anything different. This matter-of-fact mentality allows us take the same approach to all situations. And the flow that we have developed will remain unaffected and intact even in situations that once were "special" or important.

TURNING IT OVER: SEE IT, FEEL IT, TRUST IT

Less and less do you need to force things
until finally you arrive at non-action.
When nothing is done
nothing is left undone

—TAO TE CHING
(AS ADAPTED BY STEPHEN MITCHELL)

"Turning it over," or putting trust in our instincts, is our ultimate goal. Just as we don't tell the ears when to hear or the eyes when to see, your natural abilities and talents will surface best when left alone. If you are physically and mentally prepared, then you shouldn't be concerned with *how* it's going to happen. You should only be concerned with *letting* it happen.

When I use the term "turning it over," I am not suggesting that you should take a passive stance toward your performance. On the contrary, when you allow your instincts to take over, they make the right decision for you. This is because you are not *consciously* trying to do anything. And when there is no conscious activity going on, you are in the best possible position to react.

Bruce Lee once said, "the less effort, the faster and more powerful you will be." By this he meant, the less *conscious* effort, the faster and more powerful you will be. By not wasting energy on *trying*, you will be more effective. I'm sure we can all remember occasions when we "weren't trying" and the ball went both faster and farther.

Once you are truly mastered, then your only concern is to let your talent do your work for you. By turning it over, you will be by-passing your thoughts and allowing your instincts to take charge. And once we learn to trust our instincts, then regardless of the situation, our performance will take on a sudden and revolutionary change—one in which our potential can be attained as a result of less effort, rather than more.

BALANCE

Balance is more than uniting the mind, body and spirit. It is a constant reminder that whatever comes into your domain should either strengthen your center, or more importantly, be returned back to the periphery without second thought.

Throughout the course of a game, athletes will go through a spectrum of emotions. It seems that most athletes find it difficult to stay on an even keel, to avoid getting too high or too low.

By using your deep breath as a "balance point," you can ensure that you will never stray too far from your center. Your deep breath will not only relax your body and trigger your mind, but it will bring you back to the moment. It will remind you that you must keep your emotions in check by staying "grounded" at all times. Your deep breathing will also serve as a "home base," a *constant* for you to return to when you feel the pull of emotion trying to take you off course.

My clients know that when they lose their concentration or become angry, and begin to "wobble" from their balance point, there are two paths they can take: 1) they can continue to "spend" their energy (focus) on the lingering effects of frustration or disappointment, or 2) they can let go of the situation and "gather their focus" for the next action or play.

Learning how to "let go" of difficult situations and gather your focus, rather than spend it on negative energy (that is already a part of ancient history), will allow you to stay balanced.

TRANSCENDING TECHNIQUE

"If one truly wishes to master his art, technical knowledge is not enough. One must transcend technique so that the art becomes an

'artless' art, growing out of the Unconscious."

—D.T. SUZUKI

When a student finally obtains his degree from a University, he is ready to enter the work market. He has spent innumerable hours on term papers, home work assignments, mid-terms, and internships. As a graduate, he has "mastered" the theoretical, philosophical and practical basics of his specific field.

But does this background, this technical knowledge guarantee that he will be a success at his job? Does it mean he can translate theory into action? An artist may know the principles of design or color and still not be a great artist. A musician may be able to read notes and still not be a great musician. Likewise, an athlete may be proficient at every aspect of his game and still not be a great athlete.

Almost every manager and coach in professional sports is proof of that. They probably all know their fundamentals better than anyone, but how many of them, as players, made it into the hall of fame? Obviously, *technical knowledge is not enough.* One must be able to turn that technical knowledge into a fluid, effortless performance. One must be able to *transcend technique*, to go beyond one's technical skill, to allow one's Unconscious talents to take over, to make one's performance and "artless" art. This is the difference between a skilled athlete and a great athlete.

Of course, it goes without saying that we must master our mechanics first. We cannot type unless we first learn the keyboard. We cannot drive a stick shift automobile, without first learning how to mesh the gears with the clutch. But technique is only a starting point. Unconscious improvisation is the finishing point.

PLAYING FOR THE JOY OF PLAYING

Satisfaction comes from the passion of one's undertaking, rather than the material rewards that follow.

Vincent Van Gogh is recognized today as one of the greatest artists of all time. But while he was alive, he received no recognition and died ridiculed and penniless.

Despite his critics at the time, Van Gogh continued to paint. He couldn't help it; his creative impulses and passion compelled him to keep on applying brush to canvas. It didn't matter that he was poor and starving, indoors or outdoors, in Holland or in the south of France. Circumstances were of no importance to him. Consequences did not exist for him. Van Gogh painted simply for the joy of painting. His self expression was all that mattered.

Unfortunately, too many of today's athletes are motivated by reasons *other* than inward satisfaction and personal fulfillment. Because of enormous salaries and the barrage of publicity given to athletes in newspapers, magazines, radio and television, today's athlete has a lot on his mind besides the game.

With money, fame and prestige at stake, the *innocence* of the game has been lost, and athletes now find themselves performing for every reason but the right reason: to satisfy themselves.

What today's athletes don't realize is how important self-satisfaction is to staying in the flow. When your sport is "a job," you don't look forward to being there, you don't look forward to all the preparation involved, and you don't look forward to the pressure that comes with the performance itself. Not only does your attitude show through, but you become weighted down with left brain considerations. You are always aware that you are being judged, and if you fail at this at-bat, at this shot, at this tackle, your market value goes down.

Only until you can play without worrying about fame or fortune will you be able to realize the joy of the moment.

A Final Word

Going with the flow occurs when the athlete becomes so immersed in his performance that he ceases to think. When the athlete is no longer cued by his conscious will, the right movement or action seems to come by itself, effortlessly. The game is playing the athlete as much as the athlete is playing the game. As in the case of a man riding a horse, we can no longer decipher if the man is riding the horse, or the horse is riding the man.

Once this transformation takes place, the athlete will begin to merge with the elements around him much like fuel that transforms into fire, and he will no longer play "at" the game, but become part of the game.

CHAPTER 8

Life Management: Philosophy off the Field

If you don't have it together away from the field, then surely you won't have it together on the field.

Although many of us think of ourselves as "athletes," we must remember that we are human beings first. Although we spend a significant part of our lives on the playing field, we spend the majority of our life *away* from the playing field. Just as our performance *on* the playing field influences our life *away* from the playing field, what we do *away* from the playing field influences our performance *on* the playing field.

In this chapter, we will look at those forces that are trying to disrupt our focus *away* from the playing field, and what we can do to overcome them.

WILL VS. RESISTANCE

All of us at one time or another have taken up a new hobby or craft. Whether it's learning to play a musical instrument, taking an art class, or implementing a new exercise program, we attack our new interest with passion, drive and determination. This burst of energy is the result of what I have termed our *Unconscious Will to Grow*

But what happens when the initial novelty wears off?

Unfortunately, our *Unconscious will to grow* is confronted by Laziness. Because growth requires effort, sacrifice, and may even be painful at times, laziness looks for the easy way out. And while our *Unconscious will to grow* continues to push us forward, laziness urges us to take the path of least resistance. Thus we are caught in a struggle between our Unconscious Will to Grow (will) and laziness (resistance).

LAZINESS: THE SUPREME OBSTACLE TO STAYING FOCUSED

In Chapter 5 we saw that Laziness is a learned behavior. It is part of the conditioning that has taught us to take the easy way out, to look for the "quick fix," to seek pleasure and avoid pain at all costs. It is this conditioning that has taught us to put leisure ahead of truth. It is this conditioning that impedes our *Unconscious will to grow* by appealing to our intellect rather than our intuition, our ego rather than our spirit. Is it any wonder that most of our endeavors are aborted in the first month or so?

Laziness, along with *procrastination* (the delaying of responsibility), *rationalization* (the justification for not taking responsibility) and *denial* (the failure to acknowledge responsibility), are the prime saboteurs of man's attempt to not only seek change for the better, but also to *maintain* this change, including the commitment to stay focused.

STRATEGIES FOR STAYING FOCUSED

If we are to *stay* focused, we must realize that initial motivation alone cannot overcome the inevitable forces that are trying to take us out of our focus. We must supplement our *Unconscious will to grow* with trust, discipline and perseverance. We must prevail where we once gave up, persist where we once gave in.

While our initial burst of energy helped us *get* focused, *staying* focused will be the real challenge, for *staying focused* demands a lifelong commitment to take the path, not of least resistance, but of *more* resistance.

The following strategies are designed to help us maintain our focus. They are all geared to act in accordance with our *Unconscious will to grow* and to bring ourselves back to the *innocence* of the moment. They will develop a trust in ourselves to go against the grain, to stay with truth, to *keep* our focus in an unfocused world.

These strategies will be presented in three sections. The first section will provide strategies to enhance your "A" state focus. The second section will discuss the importance of your mental training in maintaining your "A" state focus. And finally, "Cycles" will show you that your "A" state awareness and your "B" state training will begin to compliment each other, creating a "whole" that is greater than the sum of its parts.

Part I: "A" State Strategies

Silencing the "familiar"

A university professor, considered very clever and astute, came to a monastery to inquire about Zen.

Nan-in, a Zen master, greeted the professor by offering him some tea. Nan-in poured his visitor's cup full, and then continued to pour even after the tea began to overflow. The professor watched until he could no longer restrain himself. "It is over full. No more will go in."

"Like this cup," Nan-in replied, "you are full of your own opinions and judgements. How can I teach you Zen unless you first empty your cup, and open your mind?"

Though our intention is to see things with an objective mind, we may still find ourselves falling prey to our old *familiar* patterns of thought. Due to the comfort and security we feel with the left hemisphere of the brain, and the place of authority we have given our "thinking," it is difficult to ignore our "thoughts." But throughout this book we have seen how thoughts are nothing more than an "echo" of "all we've been told and all we've seen," random dialogue that is often more irrational than rational.

If we are to stay focused, we must have the skill to *inactivate* the familiarity of our preconceived ideas or notions so that each new experience can be viewed objectively. Without this objectivity, the present moment is nothing more than a repetition of something that has already been seen or experienced. In a sense, we must "suspend thought" or *silence* that part of our self that is accustomed to filling the subjective world within us.

By putting our opinions on hold, we can keep a neutral attitude and absorb all situations without jumping to conclusions. We can see each moment objectively.

"Silencing the familiar" will enable you to make the transition from subjective to objective. Once we learn to *silence* our learned prejudices and biases, new situations and events will not be "tainted" by old ideas. This "awareness" allows you to welcome all occasions with freshness and spontaneity.

Although we have been hypnotized by our past thoughts, we must realize that they are nothing more than "temporary mental constructions." We should not try to hold on to them or reject them, but let them alone as they rise and as they cease. Then, and only then can we hear our intuitive voice without the dilution of our preconceived opinions. Only then will our actions be based on the here and now, and not on the past or future.

STAYING IN THE MOMENT

"Time is not a line, but a series of now points."

—TAISEN DESHIMARU

Two monks were traveling together down a muddy road during a heavy downpour. As they approached a river bed, they saw a lovely girl stranded at the foot of the river because she had wounded her leg. One of the monks, Tanzan, at once offered the girl assistance and carried her across the river.

Later that evening, as the monks arrived at the lodging temple, Tanzan's companion Ekido could no longer restrain himself. "We monks don't go near females," he told Tanzan. "It is dangerous. Why did you do that?" To this Tanzen replied, "It seems that I have left the girl back at the river, while you are still carrying her."

Unfortunately, most people go through their entire lives without realizing the essence of the moment. Most Westerners are more concerned about where they've been or where they're going than where they are. Immersed in a whirlwind of plans, appointments, things to do, places to go, people to see, Westerners tend to rush through whatever they are doing, so they can get to tomorrow today. They are so busy reliving the past or looking forward to the future that they are numb to the present.

But we cannot change the past and we cannot predict the future. The past is simply a collection of selected memories—the future, a subjective speculation of the unknown. The only time we can control is the time that exists in this moment. In fact, nothing exists *outside* of this moment, for time can only be measured in terms of where we happen to be right NOW.

Put rather simply, if you're in this moment then you can't possibly be anywhere else. If you are worrying about what *is* happening, you cannot be worrying about what may or may not happen. If you stay in the moment, your attention will be undivided, your attention sincere, and *all* energy can be channeled into the task at hand.

When washing dishes, wash dishes.

Staying in the moment helps promote natural (Unconscious) responses to life's situations because, when in the moment, there is nothing else to think about. Distracting thoughts or worries will quickly dissipate because they are not relevant to the task at hand. Once you understand this basic reality, all of your actions will be based on the here and now, and not on the past and future.

THE THREE P'S: PATIENCE, PERSPECTIVE AND PERSEVERANCE

Nothing of value comes easily. Because we, in the West, have grown accustomed to living by the "rules" of society, we are accustomed to quick results and immediate returns. But the Unconscious cannot be rushed. The changing of the guard from the old to the new is a gradual process that takes time. Getting focused required tremendous effort. *Staying focused requires tremendous patience.* If we are patient, things will happen when they are ready to happen. We cannot force the natural course of events. The snake will shed its skin when it does.

Perspective provides us with the ability to see things objectively, in spite of the deceptive dialogue of our left brain. It gives us the insight to know what plan of action is the *right* plan of action. Even though our left brain is eager to act on pre-set thought patterns, perspective will allow us to break through these old thought patterns by questioning the *validity* of these thoughts.

Finally, because we are making a dramatic change in our life, because we are challenging our secure thought patterns and taking the path of *more* resistance, because we are incorporating a new philosophy of not only sports, but of life. We must expect old habits to creep into our everyday existence. It would be unrealistic to assume that years of conditioning would simply go away overnight, even though we have found a better approach to life.we must expect to go through times of doubt or uncertainty. *Perseverance* will allow us to get through those times. We must remember that life is a series of ups and downs, but tough times, like slumps for an athlete, come and go. We must remember that all problems are temporary phases—that they are simply part of the journey. If we keep this perspective, then we will have the courage to work through our tough times and stay on our chosen path.

RESPONSIBILITY

It is said that ultimately, we are performing for ourselves. If we succeed it should be our own doing; likewise, if we fail we must take full responsibility for our actions.

Anyone can handle success. But the true winners in life are those who can take responsibility for their actions, even in the face of adversity.

Most of us have had the experience when driving a car of having another driver cut in front of us. We usually react to this by honking, cursing, or making an obscene gesture.

Unfortunately, this irrational reaction magnifies the problem rather than eliminates it. Instead of seeing the situation in its proper perspective, we have created tension, stress, and anger. Whether the other driver had a good reason to cut in front of us, or whether he or she was just using poor judgment, *it doesn't benefit us* to get so upset over a split second incident that is over as quickly as it occurred.

What it comes down to is this: our focus is our concern, and getting angry only serves to undermine it. A focused person realizes that the other car and driver hasn't created the problem; it is our response that has created the problem. As long as we remain calm and cool, there is no problem. It is our *learned reaction* to adversity that is the issue and *not* the adversity itself.

By taking responsibility for our actions, it no longer becomes a question of right and wrong, but rather, how we are going to deal with the situation. In the case of the focused person, decisions will be made which strengthen his focus rather than disrupt it. This can only be accomplished when he is prepared to see his reactions as part of the solution.

Staying focused will require you to come to terms with the fact that you are responsible for *all* of your actions, and that you must accept rather than *avoid* responsibility.

BIG EARS, SMALL MOUTH: THE ART OF LISTENING

"The quieter you are the more you can hear."

—BABA RAM DASS

It is no secret that most of us like hearing ourselves talk. After all, who doesn't enjoy expressing his opinion or sharing his knowledge? But too often we are so interested in what we have to say that we forget to listen to what the other person has to say.

Listening is perhaps mankind's most underrated skill. By listening I don't mean just keeping your eyes on the other person's face, but really *hearing* what the other person is trying to tell us. Too often we pretend we are listening, when in fact, we are simply waiting for our turn to talk.

When speaking, one should speak. But when listening, one should listen.

As part of staying focused, it is important to be a good listener. Listening helps us broaden our horizon, develop new insights, and re-evaluate opinions we already have. If we limit our knowledge to what we already know, we will stay trapped in a very small place.

Listening not only helps *us* grow, but benefits the speaker as well. If people who are speaking know you are really hearing them, it gives them a good feeling about themselves, and about you. Therefore, they are more willing to listen to what you have to say. Thus, listening creates true communication between people, an opportunity for both parties to *learn* rather than teach.

TREAT EVERYONE AS AN ALLY

Outside of perhaps the playing arena, we should view all people as teammates. Then, we would no longer have to defeat anyone.

Another symptom of the Westerner's competitive nature is that we are all suspicious of one another. As a result of our "survival of the fittest" mentality, our "guard is up" and we have lost our trust in people.

We are also quick to stereotype individuals. Often, we judge people on superficial criteria without getting to know them. We mistake their *image* for their *substance*. We set up walls and barriers between us, classifying people as those we want to know and those we don't want to know. But is this conducive to our focus? Does classifying people as "potential" ally or enemy benefit us in any way? The clear answer is no. In fact, if we look at the laws of nature, we see that one of its most essential and universal principles is *harmony*.

Harmony, or the natural adaptation of parts to each other, is a force working to keep things *in order*. It is a principle that is so fundamental to the evolution of life that without it, life as we know it would cease to exist. Without the harmony between the body's cells, we would not be alive. Without the harmony between matter and motion, the force of gravity would not hold us in place. Without the harmony between people, the world would be in chaos.

In contrast to the beliefs of a separatist Western culture, Easterners believe that there is a force that is trying to bring people together. Carl Jung called this force, the "Collective Unconscious." Jung was convinced that all individuals possess common or shared "codes" that are identical in nature. He believed that beneath our *personal* Unconscious lies a deeper Unconscious in which all human beings are connected. Interestingly enough, Jung believed that the "Personal Unconscious" is nothing more than a superficial cover that rests upon the deeper bed of the "Collective Unconscious."

Although the materialistic and competitive nature of the West has worked to alienate us from our fellow human beings, Jung's "Collective Unconscious" reminds us that our fellow men and women are *components* in our life, rather than *opponents* and that there is a common link among people—a force that is actually trying to keep people in harmony.

Staying Focused will ask you to look for the *cooperative* component in all people, even those who may be irritating or annoying. When you can see people as allies instead of enemies, pessimism will be replaced by optimism.

DISCIPLINE

Although an entire chapter was devoted to the role of discipline in *getting* focused, it's important to mention it again because of its relationship to *staying* focused. As you will recall, discipline, or self control, is the antithesis of laziness. Since laziness is the main saboteur of staying focused, it is necessary to integrate the principles of discipline into your daily life. These principles will be a constant reminder to see the Truth and take the right action at all times no matter what the cost.

By repelling counter-productive thoughts, making black and white decisions, and leaping into action, discipline will allow you to challenge your lazy tendencies.

DEEP BREATHING AS A HOME BASE

Most of the strategies we have discussed in this chapter require conscious intervention. But let's not forget the most powerful tool of all: our Unconscious.

Earlier, I stated that as your breath goes, you will go. What I meant by this is that the role of your breath is so fundamental and influential to your state of mind that your breath is a constant measure of your focus.

Diaphragmatic breathing, due to its physiological benefits, has a "carry-over" effect into your daily life. This occurs because once your body has adjusted to this style of breathing, it becomes unnatural for you to breathe through your chest. Once your diaphragm has become accustomed to "receiving" air on a consistent basis, your breath will do everything in its power to remain long and deep. It will try its best to resist tense or stressful situations because your breathing has found its *home base*. It has found its place of business where it can carry on all operations in the most productive manner possible.

Therefore, by taking an exaggerated deep breath, you will: 1) release the tension in your body and relieve the thoughts from your mind, 2) bring your entire focus back to the moment—since nothing else can be of more value than this moment, and finally, 3) be reminded, on both a conscious and an Unconscious level, to slow things down and look inward.

Thus, regardless of the situation, your ability to re-focus is only a single breath away.

Part II: Mental Training Revisited

Mental training is always an opportunity and never an obligation.

Up to now, we have concentrated on strategies to be used to stay focused in your "public" or "A" state time, but let's not forget the importance of your "private" or "B" state time, for your daily mental training techniques are the *catalyst* for staying focused in your public time.

As we saw in Chapter 4 (Meditation) and Chapter 6 (Mental Training), two twenty-minute sessions in the comfort of your own home will give you the opportunity to clear your mind, collect your thoughts and set the stage for the remainder of your day. In fact, without this private "B" state time, the chance of maintaining your focus based solely on your "A" state strategies is not very likely. Therefore, *you must make it a priority* to continue to find time on a daily basis for mental training.

But finding time may seem more and more difficult. Because of our tendencies to fall back into old habits, and because finding time takes planning and sacrifice, mental training may begin to seem like an obligation.

But nothing could be further from the truth. Seeing mental training from this standpoint is to miss the essence of this book. For mental training provides a space for you to be with yourself. It is a time to quiet your mind, to understand your true nature and to replace negative energy with positive energy. Mental training is your arena for growth. It is the only place you can go where you are free from the obligations and demands of a stressful society.

Part III: Cycles

We now see that staying focused is a two-sided approach: mental training for your private time, and "A" state strategies for your public time. But what would happen if we could transfer the calmness and clarity of our "B" state *into* the turbulence of our "A" state?

In fact, that is exactly what will happen as you continue to synchronize your daily mental training with your "A" state strategies. "B" state and "A" state will begin to "work off" each other. As your "B" state "grounds" you and establishes your daily focus, "A" state strategies will serve as a second wave to fortify that focus. As "A" state strategies fortify your daily focus, your "B" state sessions will become deeper and richer. In a sense, "A" state and "B" state will become partners, each one helping and supporting the other.

Cycles is this merging of both "A" state and "B" state. It is the union of two cooperative forces that will have an increasingly positive effect on both your "A" state and your "B" state.

As these two states begin to have a greater impact on each other, your "A" state will begin to take on the characteristics of your "B" state. Your mind will be clearer, your breath slower, and your focus stronger. In effect, you will have brought the "comforts" of your private space into your public arena. Your "B" state, or your most natural state of mind will begin to displace learned "A" state tendencies. This is what is meant by bringing the Unconscious to conscious. It is nothing more that an *extension* of your "B" state into your "A" state.

The benefits of a productive "A" and "B" state help create a cycle that is greater than the "sum of its parts." By bringing our Unconscious to conscious, we create a union of our private time and our public time. This integration helps us stay focused *at all times.*

A FINAL WORD

In this book, we have learned the reasons we are not focused, we have learned the strategies of becoming focused and staying focused, and now the rest is up to you. You can put this book on the shelf and continue on in your old ways, or you can keep this book at your side and move on to a more fulfilling life on and off the field. Your future is in your hands.

I hope you choose Getting Focused and Staying Focused.

Epilogue

Tzujan: Leaping Into Action

There is scarcely a person in the Western world who has been able to escape the limitations imposed on him or her by our fast-paced, stress-filled environment. In a society dominated by over-thinking, methodical planning and mechanical action, the spontaneous nature of the mind has been thwarted. Our instinctive and Unconscious being has been alienated by our thoughts. As a result, our actions are contrived, our spontaneity, restricted.

Tzujan is another word for *spontaneous action*. It is the way in which the Universe operates. It is also the way in which our Unconscious manifests itself. If we are to be as natural as the blowing wind, the falling rain, then we must learn to trust our Unconscious, unconditionally. And when we hear the unmistakable voice of Truth, we must not hesitate, deliberate, or analyze, but *leap into action*.

A Coaches' Manual

The mental training program set forth in this book can easily be adapted to a team situation. This section of the book is for coaches who wish to implement this program for their team. A word of caution, however. Mental training, like physical training, must be done on a *daily* basis. If you wish to reap the benefits of your mental training program, you must be diligent about setting aside twenty minutes every day for your team's mental workout.

By consistently supplementing your physical practice with mental practice, you will ensure your team is not only physically fit, but mentally fit. A team that is mentally prepared is not only less susceptible to mental distractions and pressures, but will play at a peak level on a *consistent* basis.

Specifically, this program will:

- provide your players with a private "space," a hide-away of sorts, to let go of their daily problems and worries and clear their mind;

- help bring their focus to their immediate concern and goal—*today's* practice (or game);

- allow players to develop their mental skills (i.e. concentration, discipline, confidence) so that game days no longer feel like a performance without a rehearsal;

- give them a pre-practice ritual that will get them into the habit of a pre-game ritual. Since players notoriously have too much time on their hands prior to the start of a game, they will now learn to use this time to their advantage.

IMPLEMENTING THE MENTAL TRAINING PROGRAM

Where

Although it is ideal to conduct mental training in a natural out-
door setting, it is often not practical due to the unpredictability
of the weather. Therefore, it is much more reliable to train indoors where the environment can be controlled.

Any indoor facility is acceptable if it is either carpeted or has
mats. Weight rooms and gymnasiums are two such places. Even
classrooms can be used, but they can have an adverse effect on
players due to their association with an institution rather than a
sports environment. Regardless of whether you train indoors or
outdoors, the key is consistency; to train in the same place every
day so that your players associate this place with mental training.

PREPARING THE TEAM

Before implementing the program, be sure you have given your
team a detailed overview of the entire program including its
purpose and why it works;

- The purpose of mental training is to become focused so that
  you can remain relaxed and confident under the most pressure-filled circumstances;

- Why does it work? Our minds are so full of mental congestion that we have lost touch with our natural instincts. Mental training will help us clear away this congestion, and build
  on our muscle memory so that we can play effortlessly and
  spontaneously on a more consistent basis.

At the first session, you should also include the following concepts:

- What is mental congestion and where does it come from?
- The theories of the right brain/left brain
- The effect of the environment
- The meaning of "Mastering Yourself"
- The concepts of "A" state and "B" state

Once players believe that mental training will dramatically improve their performance, even those who are most skeptical will give mental training a chance.

FACILITATING

As the person who will be talking the players through each session, try to use a soothing voice by lengthening vowels and softening consonants. Present the program over a number of days. This will allow your players to absorb the information without getting bogged down. Spend a few days on each step, and be sure each step is mastered before moving on to the next. Remember that this is a cumulative program, so that each exercise will be incorporated into the following exercises.

As the facilitator of this program, it is important that you understand the Mental Training Process thoroughly. Be sure you have reviewed each step before presenting it. The following is a guide to aid you in your presentation. If you have any problems, please refer back to Chapter 6.

STEP 1: FRAME OF MIND/"LETTING GO"

Goal: To learn how to relax by letting go of all conscious thought; to go from "A" state to "B" state; to bring the players' focus to the present moment

Duration: 3 minutes

Exercise: Assign your players a specific spot on the grass or floor, and then give them a few minutes to "wind down" and establish their space. This is easily done by telling them to imagine that there are borders around the area they are lying on (the patch of grass or the floor). Tell them that this space is their own private island in some distant land, a space that is free of problems, worries and stress.

By imagining an island, your players will symbolically associate the isolation of their island with isolating themselves from their worries or concerns. On their island, they can do anything they like. They can create forests, rivers, animals and climate. They can fish, surf, lie in the sand, walk in the forest. They can have free reign over this place. Ask them to be as creative as possible: to be very detailed by appealing to their senses and emotions. They should try to hear the sounds of the ocean; feel the warmth of the sunlight; experience the joy of being at peace with themselves.

After two or three minutes of imaging their island, ask your players to make their break from "A" state to "B" state. ("A" and "B" state will have already been explained).

Once they are in "B" state, have your players tune into their breathing. This will not only take their focus off their mind's "chatter," but will allow them to make a smooth transition to Step 2.

STEP 2: DEVELOPING THE BREATH/CONCENTRATION

Goal: Controlling the Breath

Duration: 5 minutes

Exercise: Repeat Step 1. Then have your players observe their breathing for a few minutes until it begins to find its own rhythm. Explain that the easiest way to do this is to be as passive as possible. They only need to *observe* their breathing; they don't have to try to *do* anything. If given a chance, the air will breathe them.

Direct their attention to the stomach region and ask them to try to *soften* this area. Remind them that the exhale should be as long as possible, dispersing an equal amount of oxygen throughout the entire exhale. Continue to talk them through the technical process of *exaggerated breathing* until they have taken at least ten quality Exaggerated Deep Breaths.

Exaggerated Deep Breaths will play a significant role in the Mental Training Process. Besides clearing the mind and relaxing the body, it also marks the start and finish of the Mental Training Process. (See Chapter 6 on Exaggerated Deep Breaths).

Though some of your players may find it monotonous to remain focused soley on their breathing, they must understand that *each* breath is symbolic of their intention to become focused and stay focused. Thus, each inhale and each exhale must be done deliberately and with their full attention.

A positive suggestion like "calm," "loose" or "focus" on the exhale will support their concentration and accelerate the relaxation process.

STEP 3: SPORTS ENVIRONMENT

Goal: Creating the comforts of the playing field (General)

Duration: 3 minutes

Exercise: Repeat Steps 1 and 2. As the players concentrate on their breathing, they'll find their minds beginning to clear, their concentration heightening and a deeper level of relaxation. This is an ideal mind-set for the playing field. And that's exactly where we are going.

After taking them through their last series of deep breaths, ask your players to shift their attention to the playing field. Ask them to recreate the surroundings on the playing field. As with their island, they should be as detailed as possible, appealing to all their senses. For example, a baseball player should *feel* the cool breeze, *see* the plush green grass, light brown dirt and snow white bases, and *smell* the chalk and leather.

The idea is to make the environment look and feel as realistic and *comfortable* as possible.

If Step 3 is done correctly, athletes will enter into their environment with a calm and relaxed mind...a mind-set that will be reflected in their performance.

STEP 4: NARROWING THE FOCUS

Goal: Removing peripheral distractions

Duration: 3 minutes

Exercise: Repeat Steps 1, 2 and 3. Each player has now turned the playing field into a comfortable environment. However, there is one more concern that we must address before moving onto the Visualization phase of the process. It is what I refer to as peripheral distractions.

Peripheral distractions are distractions that usually do not exist on the actual playing field (although fellow coaches and players *can* affect the player's performance). Instead, they most often occur in the stands in the form of fans, media, scouts, recruiters and family. If the players are to focus on the task at hand, they must learn how to eliminate these peripheral distractions.

Narrowing the focus, or "Blackening In" the periphery, is a concept that will allow each player to remove the stimuli that is on the periphery, without *trying* to "block" them out (blocking things out is a sure sign that the distraction is still occupying the mind). One way to blacken-in is to imagine that the playing field is a screen in a movie theater, and the stands are the seats in the theater. Then all you have to do is "drop" the house lights and the only thing that exists is the screen (the playing field).

Narrowing the focus is a two-pronged approach that will eliminate the player's peripheral distractions (outside of the playing arena) while confining the player's focus to a particular area of his or her game (hitting, throwing, shooting, swinging). The elimination of these "general" distractions is a prerequisite to Visualization.

Step 5: Visualization

Goal: Honing in your skills

Duration: 5 minutes

Exercise: Repeat Steps 1, 2, 3 and 4. Now that your players' minds are clear, relaxed, and in the comfort of their playing arena, they are in an optimal state of mind to begin Visualization exercises. Visualization, or the mental rehearsal of a specific skill, will leave a lasting impression on the circuits of their minds. In theory, Visualization is mental muscle memory and is no different from physical muscle memory. It will allow your athletes to either strengthen a specific weakness, or fine-tune a specific skill. However, unlike physical practice, Visualization can always be done under the most ideal conditions.

Before the session begins, have each player decide on a particular aspect of his or her game that he or she wants to work on. Then bring your players to the comforts of the playing field and set them loose to "practice" whatever they have chosen. Before they begin, however, remind them that quality is always more important than quantity (See Chapter 6).

Step 6: Concluding the Training Session

Goal: Finishing strong; concluding with the right attitude

Duration: 3 minutes

Exercise: Repeat Steps 1, 2, 3, 4, and 5. When the twenty minutes of mental training is over, you'll want to make sure that the players finish their session in a gradual manner. They've just been in a very comfortable and relaxed place and the last thing you want to do is rush them back to "A" state.

Bring them back to the moment by having them become aware of their breathing again. Explain to them that each deep breath is a signal that the session is coming to a close; that they are returning to the present moment. Always use this "wake up" time to remind the players of the benefits of their session: namely, that they are rejuvenated, alert and focused. These suggestions will set the tone for the ensuing practice or game.

A Final Note

Mental training is like anything else. The more you do it the easier it becomes. Although some players may be skeptical at first, if you present the training program with any degree of consistency, players will immediately notice an increase in concentration and a decrease in distractions. Good news travels fast and even close-minded players will feel that if they don't participate, they will be missing out on a golden opportunity to improve their game.

For Players Only

GAME DAY: PRE-PERFORMANCE SESSIONS

Athletes often find themselves with "too much time on their hands," or "nothing to do" just prior to game time. The pre-performance sessions presented in this appendix will not only help occupy your time, but more importantly, will allow you to clear and prep your mind for your upcoming performance. Nothing is more important than your frame of mind just prior to performance.

A pre-performance session is nothing more than a mini "B" state. By going through a condensed version of your normal "B" state, you will be more prepared for your game or match for several reasons:

- your mind will clear thoughts rather than create them,

- due to the control of your breathing your body will be less affected by common pre-game nerves,

- your concentration will intensify as you "blacken in your surroundings" and visualize some "bread and butter lanes," and

- bringing your attention to the moment will direct your focus toward your goals rather than the obstacles to your goals.

A place for pre-performance sessions can easily be arranged, since most athletes have access to either their dressing room, locker room or clubhouse. Those of you who do not have these conveniences must find some other "private space." The time for your pre-performance sessions should be twenty to thirty minutes before a game is to begin. This is your mental training time.

PRE-PERFORMANCE SESSIONS

The following program will get you on your way for the first five weeks. Then you will be ready to personalize your own program as you become more comfortable with your routine.

Step 1—Gaining Perspective

Before you begin your session, remember not to make a distinction between practicing and performing. There is no need to put on a "game face" just because you are sitting in the clubhouse with your uniform on. Remember, every day is game day, and your "game face" is always on.

Gaining this perspective will instantly reduce the majority of pre-game anxiety that is created when athletes feel the need to try harder because greater consequences are at stake. Once you have downplayed the importance of the game, your mind will be in a position to calm down, clear, and focus.

Step 2—Frame of Mind

Next, sit or lie in your designated space. Begin to bring all feelings and thoughts to the present moment. Don't be concerned about the ramifications of the upcoming game. Instead, only concern yourself with the innocence of the present moment, the calmness of your breath and the comfort of your immediate surroundings. As your mind begins to embrace the comforts of your space, begin to make your break from "A" state to "B" state. As you'll recall, this is the first step of the Mental Training Process, *Frame of Mind*.

Step 3—Breathing

As you put all of your thoughts on the shelf or simply allow them to pass like birds flying across the horizon, start becoming more aware of your breathing. If you are patient, your breathing will settle into its own rhythm. Insert a pre-determined word like loose, calm, or free to the exhale phase of your breath (remember, this "suggestion" will aid the relaxation process and give your mind something to focus on). Stay with the calmness of your breathing until your mind clears or you feel that you are absorbed by the present moment.

Step 4—Sports Environment

Now put yourself in the comforts of your *Sports Environment*, *Blacken In* your surroundings and *Visualize* those "bread and butter" skills that are most likely to be called upon during your performance. This will help your mind "lock into" those "circuits" that have been "wired" from previous mental training sessions. Although Visualization will intensify your focus, be careful not to overdo it. The key is to use a little Visualization as a reminder. You do not want to overstimulate the mind just prior to a performance.

Step 5—Finishing Strong

Finish as you would any mental training session with a minimum of Five Exaggerated Deep Breaths, emphasizing your predetermined exit word (i.e. Focused, Unconscious, or Locked In).

Step 6—Right Attitude

Since your pre-performance session is designed to remove unnecessary pre-game thinking and worrying, the emphasis should always be on *clearing* your mind. In fact, deep breathing and relaxing are the priority. Visualization should only be used to rehearse those images that have already been ingrained in your mind from previous mental training sessions.

Using pre-game time in this productive manner can greatly influence the quality of your performance. It's up to you whether you use this time to collect your focus or scatter your mind.

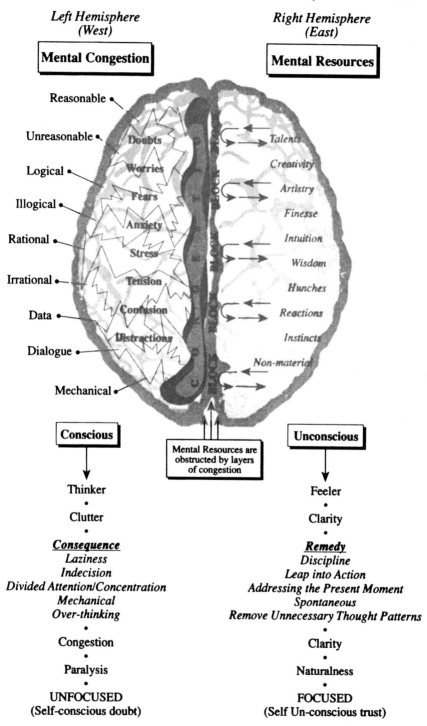

Left Hemisphere
(West)

Mental Congestion

Right Hemisphere
(East)

Mental Resources

Reasonable

Unreasonable

Logical

Illogical

Rational

Irrational

Data

Dialogue

Mechanical

Doubts

Worries

Fears

Anxiety

Stress

Tension

Confusion

Distractions

Talents

Creativity

Artistry

Finesse

Intuition

Wisdom

Hunches

Reactions

Instincts

Non-material

Conscious

Unconscious

Mental Resources are
obstructed by layers
of congestion

Thinker
•
Clutter
•
Consequence
Laziness
Indecision
Divided Attention/Concentration
Mechanical
Over-thinking
•
Congestion
•
Paralysis
•
UNFOCUSED
(Self-conscious doubt)

Feeler
•
Clarity
•
Remedy
Discipline
Leap into Action
Addressing the Present Moment
Spontaneous
Remove Unnecessary Thought Patterns
•
Clarity
•
Naturalness
•
FOCUSED
(Self Un-conscious trust)

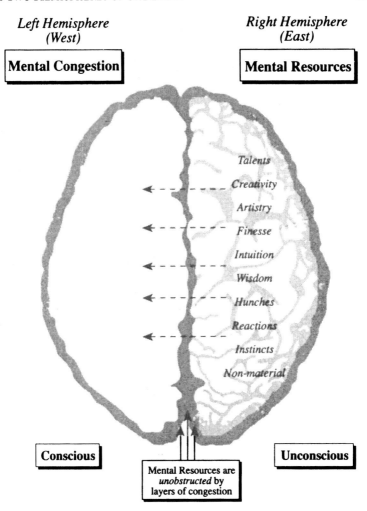

Left Hemisphere
(West)

Mental Congestion

Right Hemisphere
(East)

Mental Resources

Talents
Creativity
Artistry
Finesse
Intuition
Wisdom
Hunches
Reactions
Instincts
Non-material

Conscious

Unconscious

Mental Resources are
unobstructed by
layers of congestion

Unconscious to Conscious

NOTES

NOTES

NOTES

NOTES